Retirement Is For Sissies

Other Books by Keith Barton

Fiction

High Rise
Camouflage
The Protocol
The Reunion
Symbiosis
Low Country
Night Moves
The Kauai Connection

Non-fiction

Reflections From A Psychologist: An Autobiography
Silly Little Love Poems

Retirement Is For Sissies

✦

Or How I Survived My Job

Dr. A. Keith Barton

iUniverse, Inc.
New York Lincoln Shanghai

Retirement Is For Sissies
Or How I Survived My Job

Copyright © 2007 by A. Keith Barton

iUniverse books may be ordered through booksellers or by contacting:

iUniverse
2021 Pine Lake Road, Suite 100
Lincoln, NE 68512
www.iuniverse.com
1-800-Authors (1-800-288-4677)

ISBN: 978-0-595-44557-8 (pbk)
ISBN: 978-0-595-88884-9 (ebk)

Printed in the United States of America

This book is dedicated to the Boomers who have fought in three wars (Vietnam, Afghanistan, and Desert Storm), run Fortune 500 and small businesses, parent our grandchildren and aging parents, and lead our country at local, state, and national levels. You have accepted the challenge to make a difference with the resources given you and you make us all proud.

Contents

Prologue

Retirement conjures up various emotions and thoughts for the Boomers of today. We were born in an age of prosperity between 1946 and 1961 and have witnessed and participated in many changes that have affected our families, careers, friendships, and spirituality. The first wave of Boomers is approaching 60 this year. Some of us have already retired; still others are viewing this milestone with nervous anticipation as we enter our sixth decade of life with hopefully another twenty years to enjoy the American Dream.

In this short book I've tried to capture the burdens and opportunities that await us with humor and insight. I've offered several chapters on how to run a home business, take up new hobbies, seek friendships, volunteer, and make a difference in this world. I've relied mainly on TV and movies to capture these insights because the Boomers grew up with Howdy Doody in the 50s. Many of us are college educated thanks to the savings of our parents and our own hard work and diligence.

As the Greatest Generation (our parents) depart this life, the Boomers are left with the baton of leadership. By example we have an opportunity to show the generations behind us how to retire without giving up. Some of us will work until our last breath; still others have already slowed down to begin living without a forty-hour workweek. Those lucky enough to have made good financial decisions have already retired.

I believe our generation will be measured by what we do with our retirement. With the many advances in technology and information, we have the unique opportunity to extend our usefulness and contributions another twenty years. The choice is ours. We can hoard our resources and consume everything we've acquired to this point; or we can become stewards of our time, talents, and resources and impart by example a legacy of selflessness and philanthropy.

1

What Now?

You've got the 401k, the back porch overlooking a pond stocked with bass, the grandkids, the wife, sunrises and sunsets, so what do you do now? The only constant you need worry about is time. No more eight am meetings, traffic gridlock, stained white shirts from leaky pens, spam emails, and cute greeting cards reminding you that you're a year older. You sit on the back porch with your wife of forty years sippin' on Starbucks dark roasted Columbia blend as the sun casts an orange hue over the pond rippling with large-mouth bass enjoying the morning cool air in the Sandia mountains. Route 66 and Albuquerque can be seen in the distance as the purple shadows grow shorter and the morning dew evaporates from the Yaupon on your five-acre spread.

Mystery thrillers have replaced the business journals and magazines that for so many years professed to have all the answers on how to run a successful business. You've cashed out, hunkered in, and now sit down to the rest of your life. But some gnawing thought overcomes you and your dream retirement is not quite what you thought it would be. You planned so well for each promotion. You put the business first and now your gut tightens as you look at your watch and just five minutes has elapsed. You begin to get antsy and your right leg begins to shake. You expect the phone to ring or your computer to signal the next email, but only silence descends around you like a heavy fog.

Something seems out of kilter, but you can't put your finger on it. The wife smiles while working her crossword puzzle, still attired in a robe although the sun is near its zenith. Your fourth cup of Java tastes like peanut butter and your head is pounding like a racquetball with no place to go. You smile at your helpmate and excuse yourself. Time to check the midday news to see if you missed anything from the morning news. The phone rings and you sprint to the cordless only to find out that your bridge group has changed its next meeting to Tuesday. Your thoughts, once empirical, now become subjective and obtuse. You start to second-guess yourself—a sure sign of senility.

The mail consists of Publisher Clearinghouse Sweepstakes and assorted mail addressed to "occupant." You open the refrigerator to grab a sandwich of leftover roast beef. One Mercedes has left your retirement villa with a lone female occupant as she makes her way to her afternoon tennis lesson. You check your email only to find that your son and daughter in California are too busy to remember your birthday. You go to the medicine cabinet to pop another Tylenol as your head begins to pound like a test crash without airbags and real dummies. Your alarm sounds. The digital readout indicates five-thirty in the morning. Your heart is pounding and you suddenly realize you've had the recurring "retirement trauma."

I don't know about you but I've had this dream many times. It's a logical extension of a type A personality who has not taken the time to plan for retirement. The business magazines are replete with similar stereotypes who multi-task like an octopus on his way to a seafood buffet. You've seen the young executives with their laptops, IPODs, Dick Tracy wristwatches, and latest telecommunications toy to demonstrate to the world how busy and important they are. We've progressed from stone tablets to wireless technology and the pace is increasing exponentially. We're afraid to go on vacation without some wireless gadget attached to our ear because we might miss something important. The kids' voices sound muffled because you're connected to the office 24-7.

You've even got an alarm on your laptop to alert you to the next important IPOD casting.

You pull yourself out of bed, jump in the shower, and prepare for your final day at the office. You've slaved your way to the COO position of a large manufacturing company in the Midwest. Your parents are deceased. Your kids are running between airport terminals with their own laptops. Your wife of forty years moved to the guest room four years ago because of your snoring and your refusal to get a sleep study. You pat your only friend after his dog biscuit as you head out of your home at six in the morning, a rolled newspaper tucked under your left arm and your laptop handbag over your right shoulder. You fight the commute into Cleveland huddling your Saab in the right lane to avoid the truckers who are on their way to Chicago. You park underground in a reserved COO space that has someone else's name on it this morning.

You take the elevator up to the sixteenth floor to find that the cleaning crew had left your trashcan outside your door. Your office is littered with office depot boxes as your shelves have been cleared to make way for your successor. Fifteen years ago you took over this office from your mentor who now plays golf in Florida while dodging hurricanes. An eerie silence pervades the office suite. The balloons and gifts will arrive later, but for now you sit on your sofa and watch the sun peek through the buildings below your corner office. No meetings scheduled today; no phone calls to return; no emails to send; no plant floors to walk; no groups to process; nope, all that's on your agenda for today is to smile and pretend it's been fun.

A light appears in the next office and your administrative assistant of fifteen years greets you tearfully. She's saved your ass many a time and covered for you when the reporters were huddled outside your door ready for the next scoop about environmental snafus and anticipated litigation from the greenies and governmental players who only pretend to have real jobs. You weren't always this callous; once upon a time you were eager to grow a business that gave back to the community. But the financial gurus with their Harvard MBAs supplanted the "common good" with numbers and shareholder earnings. You remember many a meeting when you and the CFO went head to head on the future of the company. Some of the meetings were not so nice; tempers flared; egos in check; and numbers began to overtake letters. Your CEO and friend of fifteen years yielded to the same temptations that affect all leaders—succumbing to a Board of Directors who had neither the expertise nor time to dictate policy but, nevertheless, wanted to control and manage the company that you and your CEO buddy founded thirty years ago.

The office becomes a little noisier as men in white shirts and women in dark suits filter into their cubicles like bees to honey. People you've not seen in weeks rotate through your office like a turnstile gone mad. They offer you redundant euphemisms but you hear none of that. Your thoughts are elsewhere. The phone rings and one regional plant manager after another call to give you a sweet parting and more "it's been…."

Finally and mercifully the party begins with the usual exchange of war stories and "that a boys." Your boss and friend of thirty years takes the mike and presents a maudlin rendition of "this is your life." The pain is unbearable. You wished you had taken an extra Xanax before the party.

Finally it's your turn. Your knees begin to tremble and your stomach is in your throat. You begin the litany of thank-yous to both friends and enemies. You look around the room and notice how young everyone looks. Their eagerness, their optimism, their enthusiasm once belonged to you as well. You mumble words that mean nothing while everyone smiles. A final handshake from the CEO and it's over.

You carry two boxes of memories down to your Saab for its final trek home away from the skyscrapers and traffic. You call your wife on the cell phone only to get a message that she's unavailable and to leave a message at the beep. Pulling into your driveway, your companion of ten years greets you with a wet tongue and panting. You change into your walking shorts and tennis shoes and traverse the same route you and your friend have walked for ten years. Somehow this walk feels different to both of you. Your friend notices a slowness of gait, not felt before. The leash pulls you along the circular path that mimics the last thirty years of your life.

But something miraculous happens about halfway through your walk. Your companion meets a new friend who is also pulling his master through life. You begin to exchange stories and learn that your new journeyman had retired last year and was in town this week to spend time with his grandchildren before returning to his villa in the Sandia mountains. He invites you and your wife for a visit the following weekend and a tinge of excitement envelops you. You've had these feelings before: when you got married, had your first child, landed your first promotion, and assumed the COO job. But this time it was different. The person at the end of the other leash was you beckoning you to step outside your box and take a chance on life again.

2

I Hate Purple

The "Red Hat" society is an organization for women who want to greet middle age with "verve, humor, and *élan*," to quote Sue Ellen Cooper, the Queen Mother. Since 2001, chapters have proliferated to bring frivolity and spirit to women who believe humor is the best antidote to aging. They elect officers and their primary goal is to have fun. It's an excellent opportunity for women to get together and enjoy sisterhood with one another. Guys would do well to follow their example. The closest thing we have for fellowship is a Rotarian, Knights of Columbus, or Kiwanis meeting that provides service to the community but at the same time provides working networks for men who still value work and what business contacts can do for them. For those men lucky enough to belong to a men's group at church, trust and companionship evolve into deeply lasting relationships built around God, family, and service to others.

The color purple was coined in her poem, "When I Grow Old I Want To Wear Purple," by Jenny Joseph in her 1961 poem, describing aging women and the challenges they face in a society that values youth, vitality, sensuality, and mobility. It is a fact that women live longer than men and many nursing homes, assisted living, and independent living facilities are populated by women who live alone. My Godmother lives in a fine independent living program; she is quite active with her "girlfriends" and volunteering her time at the library and "country store." She lost her husband when she was 58 and she's now 86—a long time to live alone, but she swore she would never marry again after her husband died and she's kept true to her promise, including the wedding band she proudly shows to the world. I'm not taking anything away from those who pine for their departed loved ones, nor do I wish to diminish their love for their deceased spouses. But I often wonder if God intended us to live alone without the benefit of heterosexual companionship.

This is tricky ground. By companionship, I'm not implying a sexual relationship, but an intimate one built on memories and trust. Retirement today, unfortunately does not insure that both husband and wife will live together after they quit work. Divorces after thirty plus years of marriage are skyrocketing and death's door beckons the unexpected couple who has planned to enjoy life after work. I pass a sign everyday to and from work that says "live today as if it's your last." How many of us take this seriously. We've all had loved ones and friends who dropped dead of a heart attack, traffic fatality, or some mysterious infection in a hospital. No one wants as an epitaph "I wished I had spent more time at the office." Equally true is "I wish I had spent less time with my spouse." I don't mean to sound prophetic but the color purple has a biblical reference for what is described as Jesus' last days—that time between Advent and the Resurrection.

How do we desire to spend our time between the Advent of Retirement and our Resurrection from this life? For some it means traveling and reconnecting with friends. For others, it means a second career volunteering for our churches, community, and the greater good. Remember that we are called to enjoy life responsibly and unselfishly. As the songwriter said "One is a Lonely Number." I would add that "purple is a lonely color." I would want to be green in my retirement and bring life to those who are dead within themselves; to bring joy to those who are discouraged; to bring hope to those who are hopeless; to bring love to those who are without love. What are some prescriptions that might enable the Boomers to fulfill their communal obligation to serve others?

Called: I believe we are called into service for others; to put aside our selfish wants and to share our talents and time with others. The Boomers will occupy one-fifth of our population in the year 2020. What a tremendous resource to offer younger generations! Think of it; we are older and wiser if we learn from past mistakes and apply our intellect and hearts to heal broken relationships. We have gifts that are to be shared for the benefit of our neighbor. There is no excuse for "shut-ins" facing each day with a stranger when family is available. We have bought the myth of "professional caretakers" in a society where 95% will spend at least 100 days in a nursing home before they die. I'm not taking anything away from eldercare or the many CNAs who provide excellent care for seniors who have no family. But I do suggest that the Boomers have an obligation to care for our parents and extend the heritage given to us since the beginning of time.

Calmness: At seventy plus we have faced many of life's disappointments and worries. We are battle savvy about which skirmishes to stand firm and which to let go. When we were younger we were taught to "fight the good fight" and stand firm for our convictions. What often resulted were hurt feelings, broken relationships, and lost opportunities for reconciliation. How many seniors do you see get upset in a grocery store? Now, how many people between 30 and 50 do you see get upset in a grocery store? You thought that old lady driving in front of you was oblivious to the traffic. Did it ever occur to you that she has driven that stretch of road a million times and can tell you every bump and turn in the road? Older people have weathered the worries of life and have learned that 95% of the stuff they worried about didn't happen. Calmness in the face of danger or uncertainty is a commodity reserved for the old who have lived through tough times; after all, they are the survivors.

Capacity: Capacity refers to volume, space, scope, and talents. Seniors have lived a life filled with "pot holes" and they continue to patch up the bumps of life because "that's what one does." Why do you think grandparents make excellent caretakers after screwing things up as parents? They do not have the competing demands of work, family, and finances to muddle through life. It's as if a giant cataract has been removed and they now see that life is more clearly defined when there's an endpoint approaching and one's priorities become crystal clear. It is said that we spend the first half of our lives building relationships and the second half in maintaining the precious few remaining. The death of a friend or family member portends our own mortality and what precious time we have left to make a difference. The volume of life increases exponentially, not chronologically; the space extends into eternity; our scope supercedes ourselves; and our talents are to be shared, not to be hoarded. If only we knew this in our twenties—life would be so much more manageable.

Captivated: As we age we come to believe in a power greater than ourselves; for the lucky ones, we've known this since our youth; for those of us not so lucky, it takes a tragedy to remind us of our own insignificance. As we age, we become enthralled, enchanted, charmed, and captured by the vicissitudes of life and our own place in the universe. To become older is to become childlike again where we believe in miracles and magic. Peter Pan never wanted to grow up. Many of our youth today escape into drugs to avoid adult responsibilities. It's not until we're much older that innocence returns and we succumb to a force greater than ourselves if nothing more than by default. Remember Christmas morning when you wiped the sleep away from your eyes to notice that shiny new bike? Aging has a way of removing the sleep from our eyes so that we can see things that have yet to happen. To paraphrase Robert Kennedy: "some ask why things are the way they are; the perceptive ones ask why not?"

Caring: Caring for our neighbor is the great commandment in the New Testament. We've spent a lifetime of caring for ourselves and our families and we're still incomplete and out of sync with the world. Notice the next time you're with a group of older people and hear the laughter and content of their conversations. For the most part, they've quit bragging on the children and grandchildren who live ten states away. They focus more narrowly on health, ministering to others, and sharing. What a great gift seniors bring to the Boomers who are about to enter retirement?

Celebrate: Celebrate each day as a gift given to us. This role reversal takes away the pressure and worry to be happy and content. To celebrate life, as one musical artist suggests, is to "dance to the music." Take in each day as if it will be your last and cherish the moments with loved ones and friends. Fellowship does not exist unless there are at least two people willing to share life and stories. We have a choice. We can embrace the past and remain bitter; or we can embrace each day and celebrate each breath we take in. When life slows down we notice the speed bumps and potholes and can go around them.

Challenge: Life if full of challenges—the sooner we believe this the more productive we will be. Our youth today view challenge as roadblocks placed by their parents or some other authority figure to block their happiness. Growth comes only with challenge. To shy away from goals is to give up on life and to accept the status quo. This "spiral down" thinking serves only to enslave us and render us aimless and inconsequential. Instead of tuning out, tune in to taking control of your life. Nothing comes easy without effort. It's not about performance, contrary to what educators may tell you. This game of life is not learned in a classroom. It's learned on the streets, boardrooms, back porches, family reunions, and life's transitions.

Cheerful: When's the last time you saw someone scold the store clerk for mishandling their purchases? Or how about telling your bridge partner that they played the wrong card? What does this tell you about these "life should be perfect" folk who go through life as if the world owes them. This myopic thinking is selfish at best and clueless at worst. I feel sorry for folk who leave this world thinking that they've declared victory over death. A cheerful giver is contagious—whether it be time, talent, or money. Notice how people gravitate towards cheerful people. When's the last time you had a party for depressed people? Negativity and depression feed off of each other and the wound festers with each increasing perceived insult.

Changeless: Older folk tend to be more settled, consistent, reliable, steady, fixed in their beliefs and resolute. Notice at family reunions how the elders congregate with one another. There is little bravado or complaints. The arthritis is "acting up a little" or "I'm happy just to be here," are refrains heard from those who have lived life, not on their own terms but with the insight to bend with the uncertainties. Mentoring is a much underutilized resource in our world and the younger generations would do well to listen to those who have walked the path before them, to paraphrase a Native American custom.

Comfortable: Older people typically do not suffer from worry and anxiety. They are comfortable. Do not confuse comfortable with smugness or aloofness. Seniors have learned to satisfy themselves with what they have left, not what they want or need. Comfort is a commodity given to those who understand the difference between wants and needs. We spend a lifetime acquiring wants, needing little other than ourselves. It's only after a catastrophe or epiphany that we see more clearly in a dimly lit world. Next time you're in a grocery store look at the basket of an elderly couple compared to that of a younger couple. Just count the four basic food groups and see whose diet is more balanced, independent of money or health.

Complete: To be holy is to be whole—that is complete. At the risk of sounding like a preacher, notice what happens when you take away the "w" in "whole." What do you have left—that's right, a hole we've dug for ourselves that we spend a lifetime of getting out because of some addiction, insecurity, selfishness, or conceit. The "w" stands for 'we" and without a partnership with each other and with someone greater than ourselves we are rendered incomplete, inconsequential, and insignificant.

Connection: While we may live alone as seniors because of life's circumstances, we do not have to accept our fate of aloneness. There are many senior organizations and partnerships that foster sharing and connection. Our forefathers understood this when the railroad connected towns. Senior citizen centers and retirement homes can become a beehive of activity and sharing or they can become prisons for those who elect to remain isolated from their brothers and sisters. To connect is to breathe life into another human being; to disconnect is to die alone, which is the number one fear of those living alone.

Courage: Show me an angry person and I'll show you a person who's scared of losing something they never had. The serenity prayer is apropos here. God give me the courage to change the things I can, to accept the things I can't, and the wisdom to know the difference. This goes beyond any 12-step program to embrace the human existence. Courageous in death is granted to those who were courageous in life.

I hope I've given you food for thought as you approach your retirement years. Besides financial planning, we should have a "life plan" that incorporates many of the Cs mentioned above. There is nothing magic about growing older. It happens to all of us. The secret of growing older gracefully and wisely is not in the presentation but in the recipe.

3

DNR: Do Not Retire

For you Boomers who've been part of the "sandwich" generation you've undoubtedly had to take care of aging parents. Walk into any hospital and you will see DNR on the charts. DNR stands for "Do Not Resuscitate" and it's part of many wills at a time when the quality of life supercedes quantity. Not to be morose but I believe we should wear "gimmie" caps with DNR on the front. This says to our friends and family that we do not intend to retire after leaving our paying jobs and promise to enjoy life to its fullest. Forget the rocking chairs and bingo; the Boomers are not going to sit around for twenty years watching the grass grow (or concrete if you're unfortunate enough to be in a nursing home). Yep, these "boots are made for walkin" as Nancy Sinatra once said and we're cruising for the next twenty years.

So what choices do we have in spending our retirement years? I might suggest you try the following:

Take up a hobby: There are many of us who spent our school and work years doing what we *thought* we wanted to do. Now it's time to *do* what you always wanted to do. Take a course in anthropology, geology, photography, computers, and English literature, whatever makes you happy. Audit the course. You don't need grades to motivate you at this point in your life. For many of us the classroom will feel uncomfortable; we may not have pleasant memories of our school years. But the classrooms of today are high-tech and offer distance learning with the advent of the Internet and modem. Classmates may be drawn from all over the world and subjects taught by world-renowned scholars in their chosen fields.

Join a health club: I'm not talking about pumping iron three hours a day to look "ripped" with six-pack abs. At sixty, it's about flexibility and range of motion, not endurance. Fat burns and aerobics are more important than strength and building muscle. Health clubs also provide a social outlet for older singles who'd rather spend time at a juice bar rather than hanging out at a club until 2 a.m. and hailing a cab because you can't remember where you parked your car. You're also safer returning home alone rather than picking up someone who might become a stalker and give you PTSD (not to mention STD).

Start a book club: For those of you who enjoy reading, start a reading group and commit to reading a book a month with weekly discussions. Meet in each other's homes and provide refreshments. Pick a book the guys would enjoy so they get to mix it up a little. Reading improves the mind and cultivates new thoughts and ideas. Rotate book selections between fiction and non-fiction. Invite a guest speaker who might be published to add a teaching element to the group.

Adopt another senior: Use your vitality to improve the life of another senior less fortunate than yourself. Volunteer at a nursing home, assisted living, or hospital. Your exuberance will uplift their spirits. Read to someone who may have lost their eyesight or share memories with a fellow traveler.

Adopt a grandchild: There are many youngsters without grandparents living with single moms or dads who would love to have a mentor. You may not be able to keep up with them on the Game Boy or Play Station but you can teach them about world events, how a slide rule works, cooking from scratch, how to pitch a tent, hike in the wilderness without a compass, and improve their vocabulary with a game like Scrabble.

Dancing: For me the Boomers lost the opportunity to dance when rock n' roll surfaced in the fifties. The forties were part of the "big band" sound with Tommy Dorsey and Glenn Miller. Frank Sinatra, Tony Bennett, Perry Como, Dean Martin (the crooners) belted out songs we could dance to, from the jitterbug to a simple four-step. Joining a dance class to keep the juices flowing and help to keep alive those songs recorded on vinyl rather than CD will bring back memories of younger days when life was simpler and safer.

Swimming: Swimming is great exercise when the bones begin to creak and we aren't as limber as we once were. Water aerobics, water volleyball, or competitive senior swims will improve circulation and endurance. Three-fourths of our world in covered by water and many popular vacation spots offer water sports for the timid and more daring. From wetting a hook to water skiing, there are many water activities that are enjoyable and therapeutic. The only risk involved is refusing to "jump in."

RC Clubs: For the more mechanically inclined radio-controlled aircraft, boats, and cars can bridge generations. The average RC enthusiast today is around fifty and many a youngster has learned to fly RC planes from a father or older adult. Eye-hand coordination is required to be successful and a high regard for rules are well-suited for the Boomers who want to add a little fun to their lives.

Camping: I don't mean the RV or fifth-wheel crowd, but actually pitching a tent after a hike along a rugged but well-marked trail will test your scouting skills, sense of direction, navigation, and creativity. Many outward-bound camps are great team-building and character-enhancing events and volunteering to be an advisor or mentor to our younger folks would keep us young at heart and pass along outdoor knowledge to a generation mesmerized by computer games.

Cooking: Before there were microwaves we had skillets, gas stoves, and ovens. Before saran wrap and aluminum foil we had cloths to keep our foods covered. Before we had preservatives we cooked for one meal. Cooking became a rite of passage for many a woman who wanted to be a homemaker (I'm not making a political statement about women's rights and stereotyped subservience here). Cooking schools today draw a number of young people who want to offer their artistic talent and ability to create culinary delights for profit and fun. Seniors can offer much advice in this area. Recipe sharing can be a social and entertaining way for senior singles to meet and enjoy the art of cooking and breaking bread together.

Kayaking: I single out this water sport because it is easy to learn and requires strength and balance. If you're near water you can kayak. Some are light (less than 40 pounds) and can fit on the top your car. For those near a river this form of transportation takes one back to the Native Americans when canoes were used to hunt and fish. For seniors it's an excellent aerobic exercise that combines spirit, sport, and recreation with beautiful, pristine scenery to be enjoyed. I'm not talking about "white water" but a more leisurely stroll amongst nature's delights of fauna and flora.

Writing Your Autobiography: What better way to leave a legacy than to write your memoirs? I'm not referring to a bestseller, but putting on paper your life story for your grandchildren and their grandchildren. Family genealogy is popular among the Boomer crowd in an attempt to reconnect with our past at a time when families are geographically and psychologically removed from one another. With the advent of the self-publishing programs it is quite easy to have your book bound and covered. I know of one seventy-year man who used "Family Tree" software and a creative fictional mind to weave a story about how his grandparents met in Missouri in the 1820s when "badlands" and "hostels" and "prospecting" were predominant. His book was a hit at his family reunion that covered four generations.

Making Furniture: Another gentleman I knew who passed away two years ago was an engineer by training and carpenter by love. During his retirement years he managed to give each of his four daughters a dining room table and chairs, cedar chest, and rocking chairs for their infants. His garage had every imaginable tool to craft wood into these masterpieces without a nail or screw. The varnish finishes were impeccable. This same man crafted a communion table, lectern, font stand, and benches for his church as a gift of love. What craft do you wish to give back to your family and community?

Teaching: The Boomers are the first post-WWII generation to go to colleges in greater numbers than our parents. Many of us used college to avoid an unpopular war, but we brought with us an openness to question ideology and pedagogy. We protested not by dropping out but by sitting in. Many of us are still young in spirit and have since tempered our ways, but not our beliefs. Knowledge has always been a part of our lives and we owe much of our intellectual resourcefulness to excellent teachers and mentors. Why not pass along this knowledge at our local community colleges by offering a leisure learning course, online group course, or workshop for our church, mosque, or synagogue?

I hope I've given you some ideas on how to live out your retirement years that utilize your body and brain. Active learning is a wonderful gift and as stewards of this rare knowledge we have an obligation to share our thoughts and insight with the next generation. DNR should be worn proudly on our hats because by doing so we profess to others our desire to keep on living—not just chronologically but intellectually, spiritually, and emotionally. Do Not Retire should be our battle cry to those who would say that "we're over the hill." To them I say, try and catch me.

4

Take Your Viagra and Shove It

You've seen the ads on TV—an elderly couple barely able to walk sitting in hot tubs overlooking the Pacific Northwest holding hands and drinking wine. You'd think they were in Vegas and about to engage in carnal chicanery. The pharmaceutical industry has done a hose-job to make you think senior men can't find their sexuality without the help of pills. Remember this is the same guy with zits chasing skirts since he was fourteen. After strutting his stuff for forty years and groping everything that moves above the waist, you'd think he suddenly had a sexual stroke. But alas, living better through chemistry has saved his manhood and his horny wife can finally wipe that smirk off her face. Tonight's the night; lock the doors and windows; nail down the furniture; remove all objects that might interfere with two elderly folks (one with blue hair and the other with no hair) making love like they were transported back in time when heavy breathing was not associated with COPD.

Do Hollywood and the pharmaceutical companies really expect us to buy this crap? Pretty soon the Viagra, Cialis, and whatever else they invent will be available over the counter next to the condoms. Can't you see grandpa and grandson going to the pharmacy together to get some ammunition? Yep, the family that satisfies their sexual urges stays together. Just don't let junior sit in the back of the pick-up or he might embarrass himself with the neighbors watching. Geez, with the miracles of modern medicine your grandmother could get impregnated by that ole' codger you thought only knew how to rock back and forth.

Seriously now, our western society is fascinated with sexual content, innuendo, humor, and fantasies. Europeans are much more blasé about the subject and laugh at us for our adolescent preoccupation with sexual performance. The Boomers have been competing since the first grade for colleges and good jobs; now senior ads would have you think that we have to compete for sexual potency in the bedroom if we're to keep our marriages intact and spontaneous. What ever happened to cuddling, candles, cozy walks on cold evenings, snuggling under the covers, kissing the way it used to be? I think we confuse intimacy with sex. Elderly couples may have drifted apart as empty nesters but the way to arouse their interest in sex is not a pill. This serves only to glorify male potency as the only way to please one's mate. What ever happened to washing the dishes?

Gary Chapman's book on *The Five Love Languages* suggests that women and men respond to certain love languages. If one does not recognize his or her partner's primary love language then an interpreter is required to help ma and pa communicate their sexual interests and needs. (I'm not proposing a threesome here).

The first language is *words of affirmation.* Telling your spouse that he or she looks nice or whispering to them that they still are as beautiful as the day you met means a lot to those of us with receding hairlines and sagging skin. The mistake most of make in our sixties is that we assume our partner already knows everything about us, so why mention the obvious? Do this and your marriage will hemorrhage at its most vulnerable point and it's not a pretty sight.

The second language is *acts of service.* Doing the dishes, mowing the grass, putting away the wine glasses, removing the dog poop from the yard without reminders is important in the art of communication and compromise. Know your spouse's most disgusting tasks and offer your service without him or her asking and you'll be surprised at the reception you'll receive.

The third language is *physical touching.* Now men think they have this one down pat, but they totally miss the boat on this one. I said touching, not groping. Men think if they grab a boob, the wife wants to hop in the sack with them before Larry King comes on the tube. WRONG. Women like to be caressed gently; they don't want to be manhandled after dealing with grandchildren or fighting for a handicap sticker. Back rubs, massages, a gentle kiss on the nape of her neck, breathing on her back while you're cuddling in bed are the ticket to intimacy. One can have sex without intimacy, but it's nearly impossible to have intimacy without sex. Men require a refresher course at age sixty about what turns women on. Forget Victoria Secret guys. The nighties itch and they won't stay on her for long. Don't waste your money on clothes, but do spend money on fragrances, creams, bath oils, lighting, music, and desserts.

The fourth language is *receiving gifts.* Gifts are visual signs of love. The next time you pick out jewelry for your wife, guys, take her with you. There's no way to surprise her and the time together (see quality time to be discussed next) will more than make up for a surprise gift that she will most likely take back. More than money or purchases, the gift of *self* during a crisis is what will endear you wife to you forever.

The fifth language is *quality time.* Quality time is different from togetherness. Spouses can be in the same room but at totally different places emotionally and mentally. While the male punches the remote control, flipping through channels, the female might be talking to her children on the cell phone. Yes you're in the same room together, but you might as well be on different planets. Quality time, according to Chapman, is active listening and focused attention to what your partner is saying. This includes both verbal and nonverbal communication.

Try sitting next to each other on the couch with the lights dimmed with your favorite beverage while you listen to each other without interrupting, solving problems, pontificating, or speaking in robotic tones. Set aside ten minutes each night to do this and you can flush your Viagra down the commode.

Michael Gurian has written a wonderful book, *What Could He Be Thinking: How a Man's Mind Really Works*, St. Martin's Press, 2003. His book provides fascinating material using brain imaging and physiology to enlighten men on what women already know about our habits, thoughts, tendencies, and actions. It's frightening to think that men are the weaker sex when it comes to figuring out the opposite sex. Hey guys, wake up; it's not about sex; repeat after me; it's not S-E-X. You've been spending too much time at the water cooler hearing war stories on sexual conquests. Instead look at SEX with a more European view:

S is for sensual. The chase is still important, so keep your membership at the gym. Next time you bring her flowers, remove the thorns and gently brush the side of her face with the rose petal. Don't drop the flowers on the counter and expect her to get a vase and become a horticulturist.

E is for excitement. Don't bring flowers on Valentine's Day or after an argument. Surprise her when she least expects it. She's getting groceries out of the back of her SUV and you arrive in time with a rose between your teeth, snap your fingers, and the two adolescent males with zits carry the groceries in while you twirl her around in the driveway that would make every neighbor blush (of course you've already paid the boys twenty bucks to keep quiet and never tell anyone that the old man next door to them is Fred Astaire).

X is for X-ray vision. I don't mean Clark Kent high on Kryptonite, but envisioning what the woman in your life really enjoys. Take time to know her again. Pretend it's a first date and you know nothing about her. Look into her eyes while she's talking instead of the waitress. Mind your manners and be sure to pull her chair out if the wait staff has not already done so. Move the centerpiece and candle so you can see each other. Do not interrupt each other. Use the silence to study facial features, especially her eyes. Pretend that the two of you are the only couple at dinner and you'll never see these people again.

Gurian talks about male *fragility* (not fertility), a need to be *needed*, a need for *sex*, and a need to be trusted for what he *does*. The more intimate the relationship the more willing the male is willing to talk about his needs. After forty years of marriage has passed men still need to be loved, listened to, sexual companionship that keeps romance in the marriage rather than duty, and most importantly, to be trusted for what he does, especially during retirement when his job no longer defines who he is.

So turn the TV off, throw away your pills, put fresh sheets on the bed, place your favorite CD in the changer, light some candles (after taking a bubble bath together), and cozy up to that woman who still recognizes your talents, wants to be your confidante, needs you for companionship, and wants to have great sex with you.

5

Work is a Four-letter Word

Let's face it. Of all the expletives we encounter as adults, nothing is more disdainful than W-O-R-K. The Dilbert series, although a parody about work, nevertheless captures the essence of mediocrity. There is a statistical concept called "regression towards the mean" which simply put suggests that inertia wins out after all the peaks and valleys. The familiar "bell-shaped" curve shows that 68% of our workforce functions in the average range, while the remaining 32% is evenly split between "loafers" and "rate-busters."

So what's this got to do with retirement? Plenty. Two-thirds of us will blindly accept retirement as a "slowing down" process. We will trade the routine of work for the routine of retirement. You know the type. Ralph mows his yard on Mondays, takes out the trash on Tuesdays, shops on Wednesdays, plays golf with his buddies on Thursdays, might go shopping with the wife on Fridays, baby-sit the grandkids on Saturdays, and church on Sundays. Sound exciting? Maybe you'd rather have a lobotomy and join the 16% who will spend their retirement years in therapy, hating everyone who ever wronged them, complain about politicians, religious pundits, and every ethic group unlike them to justify their miserable life. Or perhaps you have decided to join the top 16% who will use their retirement years to experience new opportunities for personal growth and relationships.

Let's begin with Jack and Jill. They've just moved to "Sun City" to downsize from their five-thousand square foot home with game room, pool, and empty guest bedrooms. Their "dream home" looks identical to everyone else's dream home complete with a large informal gathering place with 10-foot ceilings and homogenous paint throughout. Mailboxes are fifty yards down the street and require a key for entry. SUVs and trucks are not allowed in garages because they are built for two VWs. Playground equipment has been replaced by shuffle board and bridge rooms at the "senior activity center." A blue-hair divorcee with a recent facelift does her best to engage five poor ladies in wheelchairs with a Glenn Miller tune while the men putter around outside with little white balls. I don't know about you, but I can't think of a more depressing way to spend my retirement years—*a la* "Stepford Farts."

Let's fast forward to another scenario. You and your wife of fifty years are finishing up your palates orchestrated by a former drill instructor from Camp Pendleton. The sweat is pouring profusely down your sagging skin and collecting in pockets that you don't want to know about. An art class is scheduled after lunch with a famous chef who is teaching your class on French cooking and presentation. Symphony tickets propel you and your wife to a showing of The Producers. You meet the cast backstage arranged by your drama teacher. Your email messages are from people you met online at a retirement website and you are sharing travel information especially developed for seniors. Now which view do you have for your retirement?

It's no secret that the retirement industry will be the next big wave to hit the marketplace. We will have more disposable income than our parents and we hopefully have developed a savings strategy to maximize returns. Figure on a compounded rate of six percent after inflation is taken into account. This is what the stock market has done over the last fifty years when all the volatility is taken into account. The question becomes: do you want to manage your own retirement or do you want someone else (like Del Webb) to do this for you. There are many who will feed you the "all in one" packages that take away any guesswork or individuality. But to we Boomers who desire to "master our own fate," this option appears lackluster. Let's see what we can come up with by using the dirty four-letter word.

W is for Will Power: To stay with the big dogs you've got to plan ahead and think big. Those of you who've run your own businesses should transition into running your own retirement company quite nicely. But you have to have the stamina and will power to actively participate in your retirement program. Figure out what you need to live on comfortably, not extravagantly. For most of us, this means "cutting back" and protecting your retirement egg. No need for the timeshare at this point; you've probably run out of weeks by now unless you have a deed to the weeks you own. Don't mess with companies like RCI that trade weeks and points. Life is supposed to be simpler. You don't want to be on your computer trading weeks two years away to go on your dream vacation. Become your own travel agency and pretend you're the CEO; plan at least two months a year away from your primary living place. Of these two months, arrange for an educational seminar that is offered at an interesting travel venue. Stay away from the tourist traps; forget Martha's Vineyard and Cabo San Lucas for your seminar site. Try your alma mater; many colleges have "back to campus" offerings for their alumni.

O is for Organization: Retirement just doesn't happen by chance. You planned for it and should be actively involved. Write a strategic plan for your retirement. Perform a SWOT analysis (strengths, weaknesses, opportunities, and threats) that will affect your retirement. Now that you're the CEO of your retirement company, you should devote at least two hours a day researching financial, social, educational, and health products that appeal to you. Buy a spam blocker for your email and eliminate all the health-enhancement crap that purports to prolong youth. Develop the habit of reading at least one "how to" book a month on retirement. Read another book a month for pleasure. Convert one of your bedrooms to an office where your laptop and wireless internet service can do the research for you. Be open to changes when opportunities present themselves. I just talked to a CPA who took his wife, son, and daughter-in-law to the Rose Bowl to see USC and UT. They went without tickets. They are staunch UT alumni and had the Will Power and Organization to plan to be at the Will Call line two hours before game time. No scalpers, no prayers—just careful planning that landed them four tickets at face value because sixty seats were sold and not used because of family emergencies.

R is for Resourceful: You need to be creative in putting together your retirement program. Choose between volunteer work, personal growth, spiritual commitment, family activities, health and fitness, and financial resources. Learn to think conceptually rather than linear; imagine you've got only one good year left and plan to cram everything you wanted to accomplish or experience in this one year without stressing out. Pacing is important. Retirement is a marathon, not a sprint. Network with like-minded retired folk who enjoy the same activities you do. The internet is filled with information and makes on line chats available.

K is for Knowledge: This key to a successful retirement is the same as for any successful venture. How-to books, magazines, articles, talk shows, and seminars at your local community college are invaluable venues to learn more about those issues affecting seniors, from prescription drug costs to nutrition, and exercise to maintaining a healthy lifestyle, so that you can benefit from all that is available. For the more adventurous there is hiking, skiing, and kayaking. I met a 71-year old last year at Snowbird ski resort in Utah who skied the black diamond slopes effortlessly. He looked fifty and was in great shape, not to mention the fact he started skiing at seven. When looking for material on retirement stay away from the trade magazines like *AARP, Men's Health and Fitness* and other similar magazines that are more about selling ads and self-promotion than providing good information.

To summarize, make retirement your full-time job. Pay yourself by investing time and energy into your new role. Remember, the W-O-R-K acronym and keep an open mind when it comes to living out your retirement years. Your life will take on new meaning and urgency, now free from the typical distractions of work and raising a family. Be generous with your time and money and focus on relationships rather than yourself. Don't leave anything to chance or you will come up short in your retirement plan. Hard work can be enjoyable as long as you keep in mind that your CEO title is very real. Treat yourself kindly and with respect for the time given to you.

6

Maturity is not Mediocrity

When's the last time you saw aging folk conquering Mt. Everest or discovering a new formula for artificial sweeteners. TV and Hollywood would have you believe that the "bold and beautiful" rule the world. John Kennedy was 43 when he was elected President, a milestone for the younger generation. Most of our elected officials today run on a platform of youth instead of experience as evidenced by the last two presidents. It appears as though obsolescence is evitable as we become older and feebler. Forget the fact that Colonel Sanders was in his seventies when he invented his "secret recipe" for KFC. Forget George Bush #41 jumping out of an airplane to celebrate his 80th birthday. Forget that his wife still is the chief consultant among the Bush Clan. Rose Kennedy was the matriarch as well as Eleanor Roosevelt for her generation.

As the first of the baby Boomers turns sixty this year (the youngest is 45), a renaissance for the "young-old" is in progress. Marketers have known this for years and can't wait for the "sixty generation" to spend some of their hard-earned cash, accumulated over four decades of hard work. The travel industry is salivating as Boomers book more cruises and excursions to exotic places. Grandma and grandpa are not content to sit at home and watch the grandkids as the WWII generation did out of sense of duty. This is not to say that the Boomers are selfish, but that they have a better grip on a balanced life and what to expect from and for themselves. We are volunteering in greater numbers for local, national, and international charities. Church membership for mainline churches is primarily those of AARP age and older. Old money is tied up with older families of established wealth from oil, land, and gas. Generation X and XY have found quick wealth in the information age brought about by computers, as evidenced by Bill Gates and Michael Dell. The dot.com bust was predicated on greed versus an understanding of what the consumer wants and expects from products and services.

Let's look at some of the reasons why the Boomers will continue to dominate business, politics, and world events.

Maturity: There is no substitute for experience. The Boomers have been overachievers since Sputnik in 1957. The space race supplanted the arms race of the 40s and talented engineers went into aerospace and business. MBAs fresh out of school were armed with Keynesian logic and international supply and demand to head up major corporations in the 60s, many of which were tied to the space and military-industrial complex. Many of NASA's patents are part of our everyday appliances such as the microwave and smaller electronic devices. As the "brain drain" begins to take place next year with the early retirement of the Boomers, many of whom have already earned more than they require to live comfortably, a void will be left in our country where intellectual pursuits are no longer valued as much as "easy money" and a breakdown of morals. William Bennett's book on the moral decline in values was pivotal in drawing attention to a decline in family and business values and core beliefs that occurred before the Enron and World.com debacles.

Now we're facing a political crisis over money laundering of political contributions in exchange for political favors. Yes it seems that Generation X and XY have been brainwashed into believing that there's a sucker born every minute. Forget about quality service and giving the customers what they want—let's give them what they *think* they need. As we crank out more plasma and LCD flat screens to an obese generation who cares little about health and longevity, we run the risk of further accepting mediocrity for maturity and excellence. When Tom Peters first authored his book on *In Search of Excellence*, in 1982, his prophetic announcement was that excellently run companies depend on a company's values and beliefs that mirror present-day culture.

Malice: Make no mistake about it. We are a meaner nation who is far different from the one our forefathers set sail for and our grandparents found new opportunities after landing at Ellis Island, Galveston, and New Orleans in the first part of the 20th century. Turn on the news and notice the number of murders, beatings, degradation, and breakdown of our families. The "tie that binds" families has been supplanted by greed and contagion mentality that "let's get ours before they get theirs." We just finished another holiday season. Did you notice how rude people were in the stores and parking lots to make sure that the perfect gift was opened under *their* Christmas tree? Drive-by shootings, car jackings, AMT murders, school shootings, missing children, and ERs filled to capacity because many cannot afford health insurance are part of our lives now.

Moral decline: It's a sorry state of affairs when our business schools have courses on business ethics. The Boomers grew up after WWII, their parents part of the Greatest Generation, and expected to contribute to the Great Society under LBJ. A funny thing happened on the way to morality—DRUGS. Make no mistake; drugs have been primarily responsible for our moral decay. Beginning with hashish and LSD in the 60s and continuing through today with Xanax bars, Ecstasy, cannabis, uppers and downers ordered over the Internet, the Boomers were the first generation exposed to drugs on a wide scale. The "me" generation was born. The politics and economics are more subtle, but the message remains the same—poverty sucks. No matter what end of the political spectrum you're on you have been exposed to drugs and have felt the insidious effects of mind-altering medications that are supposed to make us think more clearly while we live in a more anxious world.

Money: Have you heard the expression that "money talks and bullshit walks?" Witness the dot.com fiasco of the 90s. Company balance sheets show profits where there is no product or service. Remember when cooking and reading pertained to different endeavors? Now we "cook the books" to make companies look more profitable than they are. Stockholders and pension holders are duped into a feverish mentality that short-term profits are good despite the lack of a long-term strategic plan. It's not that money is evil, but that the *love* of money is evil. Does it make sense that we have overpaid athletes quitting school to invest in tax shelters while our teachers continue to draw retirement funds depleted by inflation and an uncaring public who votes for six-figure salaries for coaches and administrators rather than early childhood and special education teachers? Tom Cruise in his classic line "show me the money" from *Jerry Maguire* is now part of our lexicon. Pity that "we work hard for our money" no longer describes a generation in the pursuit of excellence.

Monopoly: A monopoly is defined as having total control over a product or service due to unfair influence or advantage. How many mom and pop stores do you frequent now? As the Wal-Marts, Walgreens, Best-Buys, and CVS pharmacies continue to develop at an alarming rate, look at what happened to your neighborhood grocery store or pharmacy. Small business development is at a critical juncture today because tax incentives are not available to the small business owner compared to major corporations. When's the last time you heard of reduced property or no property taxes to small business owners? When is the last time you saw a Wal-Mart close due to unfair competition? Big business wins because they pay Washington lobbyists the big bucks to influence legislation favorable to big business. Just witness the latest Abramson scandal.

Malaise: Obsolescence is not the enemy, it's settling for less than our best. David Halberstam wrote a seminal account of the *The Best and The Brightest* in his book of the same name. Clock watchers have replaced the industrial revolution. Manufacturing is down in the U.S. because of unfair competition in foreign countries due to lower wages and governmental incentives. Senility has replaced civility. We have managers who haven't a clue about how to manage a team or innovate. Crime has replaced ethics and legal contracts have replaced handshakes. It's not *who* you know now but *what* you know. We now spend millions of dollars protecting our companies and ourselves against trade secrets, identity theft, and corporate pirating. We now pursue quick profits to benefit a few at the top at the expense of the line worker who just lost his/her pension because the fund was siphoned off to shelter shell corporations. Mediocrity and malaise are part of the same malady—greed and laziness.

Master*:* Our country was founded by master tradesmen who apprenticed for years while perfecting their craft from glass blowing to carpentry, blacksmith to pharmaceuticals, from masonry to painting. You've heard the expression "jack of all trades, master of none." There's something to be said for mastering a skill from a learned mentor. B-schools today are quick to hand out sheepskins to newbies who haven't a clue about managing people, developing products or innovation. A master was his own boss, proprietor, teacher, and owner. Now we work for corporations beholden to stockholders rather than their own employees. We fire older, more knowledgeable workers because we can replace them with two or three younger, less knowledgeable workers. We no longer recognize the trades as we once did. The emphasis now is on international commerce, trade tariffs, cheaper labor, outsourcing, and outwitting our competition.

Merit: When's the last time you heard this word spoken at a board meeting or corporate business meeting? There was a time when merit was valued—the word stands for virtue, worth, integrity, and goodness. Pick up your local business section of the newspaper and count how many times the word merit is found in any of the articles. Chances are you will find just the opposite. Look at the number of executives under indictments for misusing and misguiding the public trust. Visionaries possess merit; they are born leaders. George Washington and Abraham Lincoln had this trait. Men and women followed them anywhere for just cause and reason. How many former Enron employees blindly accepted Ken Lay's admonition to "stay the course" while he was selling off his personal shares of stock faster than cod liver oil through a constipated child?

Mind: When the President takes the oath of office part of his charge is to affirm that he or she is "of sound mind." The litmus test for any leader is an attentive, thoughtful approach to decisions without regard for personal gain but for the "common good." Our founding fathers were mindful of this in 1781 when the Articles of Confederation were ratified in Philadelphia. We as a developing nation knew nothing of greatness before our independence from European dominance. Our greatness came from men and women willing to sacrifice self for a cause greater than their own. In times of war this is not only necessary but required. But blind allegiance has its own caveat—blind loyalty to a person rather than a cause. To sanctify a person is to give away one's freedom of choice and to belittle one's soul. Witness Jim Jones and David Koresh—or for that matter, Richard Nixon or Ken Lay. David Baldacci's books about *Total Control* and *Absolute Power* are literary testaments to the danger of leaving power in the hands of the few without checks and balances.

Mystery: There should be no mystery about how to approach one's retirement. If you have lived a life of merit, integrity, and morality, without malaise or mediocrity, of sound mind, master of your own fate, and faithful steward to your possessions, you should have no trouble managing your time and money. The decision to retire should begin the moment you enter the workforce. Financial planning is but one piece of the puzzle. Although important, finances do not insure happiness or a sense of ownership. We can decide to "muddle through" life, taking gratuitous turns in a life without purpose, or we can choose as Rick Warren suggests, *A Purpose Driven Life*, that derives from the earliest of all management principles and that is to treat others as you would like to be treated.

7

To Begin is Easy

Remember how dreadful sounding the word, "Retirement," was when your father or mother retired? My experience was fairly typical. Dad would putter around the house, learn to shop, run errands, and spend more time with extended family. He and mom would take day trips to museums, viewing the central Texas Hill Country, and fishing. As a college student I didn't notice any difference. I was too busy with my own "stuff" to notice any change in my parents' new take on life. They were not the RV type; no "fifth wheel." My mother hated camping and all their traveling during their naval tours had worn thin on them. What they enjoyed was simply a home base to entertain the grandchildren.

Times have changed. Retirement is a "blur" between working at an office and working for oneself for the Boomers. Small business start-ups and home businesses have increased exponentially in the last decade. A magazine is now devoted to small business development: *Fortune Small Business*. With today's technology one can work from their IPOD or laptop in a wireless café while sippin' on their favorite Java drink. The young "road warriors" of today work for corporations. They spend their time in airports, while the Boomer retirees work at a slower pace from their homes, gardens, beach houses, and mountain retreats.

In an earlier chapter I alluded to the fact that Retirement was WORK. Retirement can also be PLAY. But for this to happen one must be careful to PLAN, LEAD, ATTEMPT, and YIELD. Let's look at each of these in a little more detail.

Plan: Nothing happens by chance. If they do, we call these events "miracles." Planning is basic to any endeavor. Before one begins a course of action they must first have a roadmap as to where they're going. One of the first questions I ask folks who are contemplating retirement is "where do you want to live?" This seems like a simple enough question but I generally get a "deer in the headlight" response. Silence. Many people honestly haven't given any thought to where they want to live. If you play golf, do you want to retire on a golf course? If you enjoy fishing, I would assume you want to be near the water instead of Sedona, Arizona. If you enjoy the mountains, then the low-lands off the Georgia coast may not be the place for you. Get the picture?

Another aspect of planning is talking with your significant other. Many arguments ensue because of assumptions and mind reading. The wife wants to be in a small community of antiques while the husband wants to be in a high rise in a thriving metropolis. Hello! We've got a classic disconnect in communication and at least one person will be terribly unhappy in their retirement. The second aspect of planning is to communicate with your partner as similar interests and availability and accessibility of activities suitable to both. A small 18-hole golf course in an older, smaller town with calendar events throughout the year may be a welcome compromise for our assuming couple above.

Many folks want to be close to their grandchildren. This is a bad idea for one simple reason: children move when new job offers come along. Unless you want your RV parked in their driveway in AnyTown, USA, you best forget relational geography when planning where to live. Airfares are cheap compared to gasoline costs and RV rentals and you're no more than a two-hour drive to even the most remote location if you want to see your children and grandchildren. Remember this is YOUR retirement. Forget about pleasing and accommodating others; you've done that your entire life—now it's time to think about *numero uno*.

Another misconception about retirement is that you can live at the same level of income. For most of us average folk this simply is not true. If you've been to a financial advisor, then you know how much you can spend annually from your 401(k) or SEP by calculating your remaining years and dividing into your nest egg plus some interest minus inflation—typically a net gain of 6% annually to the current principal remaining. Unless you plan on winning the lottery this is all there is. It should be no surprise that seniors make up the largest bankruptcy cohort in the United States today because they overlook simple math.

Lead: No reason to quit leading when you turn 65 (or whatever makes you happy). Any motivational book has this common admonition. Be a leader and not a follower when it comes to executing your retirement plan. Be wary of glitzy ads that show obese seniors line dancing by the pool next to the golf course by some instructor four decades our junior. Stay away from Florida and California unless you've got a truck load of money you want to spend before you celebrate your first year of freedom. Leading builds on planning. You've done your research and have decided on a place you can afford. You've figured the income side of the equation but now remains the expense side. The key variable is your willingness to size down. You've dealt with sizing ever since you started work; no reason to quit when you retire.

Part of downsizing is your willingness to forego some luxuries in order to enjoy your hard-fought retirement villa in the country. You may want to offer some time in the pro shop at the register or making sure the cart batteries are charged or help out with marshalling if you want some free rounds of golf. You may volunteer at the local bookstore if you want to buy your books at cost (some 60% in savings). You may want to offer an ongoing seminar on sheltering taxable income at your local resort if you want free amenities and clubhouse privileges. The list is endless if you'll use your talents, imagination, and forthrightness to save some expenses. I know a 65-year old man who works the hardware department at Wal-Mart twenty hours weekly to defray expenses and he gets an additional 10% break on any store item.

Leadership is so important. The Boomers today are well qualified in making decisions and being resourceful. There's absolutely no reason to soften your approach when you retire. Many a volunteer organization or informal club was started with time and resourcefulness (notice I didn't say money). I often ask seniors to pretend that they own their retirement company as contrasted with managing their retirement. This offers a new perspective on accountability and resourcefulness. Any action steps not carefully planned and executed will not move you forward in your retirement and you will stagnate and become bored and disillusioned. Don't rely on others to plan your retirement. They will not be as judicious in managing YOUR money and time. If you're the CEO of your retirement plan, then YOU must be prepared to step forward with a workable plan that allows for personal growth, fun, and sharing.

Attempt: If at first you don't succeed, try and try again. This works only if you don't have a plan and you're not willing to lead your own retirement. At the risk of sounding linear and business-like, I would venture that failed past attempts were either the result of a lack of planning or effort. My rendering of "attempt" is to strive or venture out of your comfort zone. A life without attempts is a life of complacency. There should be fun and excitement in your retirement years. Did you slave sixty hours a week NOT to have fun and excitement? I've seen too many retirees play it safe and not venture out to follow their dreams. If you want to open up a bookstore and work part-time while writing the next great American novel, then do your homework and see if this is feasible. Listen to your own inner calling, that intuitive spark that ignites and excites. Many a second business was begun on intuition and follow-through.

If you're unsure about where you want to retire you might try renting while checking out the area and local commerce, business, and recreational opportunities. If Charleston, South Carolina, appeals to you, then you might rent a place in Summerville, a mere 30-minute drive from Charleston. Besides being cheaper you'll have time to view the countryside away from the tourists to gain a sense of the low country charm and ambience. If Sedona, Arizona, appeals to you, then you might try Cottonwood, a "working town" of about 30,000 folks 20 miles to the west of Sedona, before you take the plunge into your desert environment. Attempts are not measured by successes and failures but by small steps that take you closer to your goal. It's like a free look.

Yield: By yielding I do not mean give up. I use the word to mean "succumb" to your own prejudices and ego. Don't be hell bent to retire on Hilton Head Island if you're a golfer, unless you have millions at your disposal. In a spiritual sense yielding is "succumbing to a calling from God." In almost any religion works is important and sharing your retirement with others will help you live longer and happier. Be open to joining small group discussions, exercise groups, a local church, mosque, or synagogue. In this, our final chapter of life on the planet Earth, one must be willing to follow the golden rule and be of service and enjoyment to others. Be ready to share your retirement with like-minded individuals and for those of you brave enough, reach outside your comfort zone and extend greetings into a *barrio*, low-income, and people of color. Yield to that inner voice that says "take a chance" and share your time, talent, and skills with others. Unless you plan to retire on your own island, remember we already share the planet Earth.

I began this chapter with an acronym for PLAY to help the Boomers step outside their comfort zones and offer themselves to others in their retirement. In reality, one never truly retires: one chooses either to live or not live. Living implies continuing growth through faith, nourishment, resourcefulness, intellect, and intuition. To define life in stages diminishes the human experience and forces us to think of stages of development demarcated by giant chasms that must be traversed. If we look at life as a process of continuing growth and development, then retirement is one point closer to our final resting place. Remember it's not the year of your birth or death but the DASH that counts between these two arbitrary end points. Use the PLAY model for your retirement and you will enjoy a sense of ownership and accountability that allows you to *live* life rather than moving *through* life.

8

Leap Before You Creep

What's holding you back? Are you judiciously counting your 401(k) and perusing stock quotes every morning? Come on! You've spent your entire life playing it safe and now you got a "nest egg" that for most won't last through the winter. You bought the myth about retiring early and kicking back and watching the grandkids while you rock away on the front porch of your patio home. Antonio is mowing the lawn while the dog you inherited from your son shits in the back yard to help fertilize your lawn. Your neighbors can be heard on either side of you on your zero lot. A neon sign stares down on you at night from the BBQ joint across the street. This definitely was not what you pictured looking at the brochures of warm, orange sunsets over the Grand Tetons. Nope. You're mired in "Retirement Land."

The wife wants a facelift; the grandkids want lifters on their 4-wheel drive trucks, and your parents need a lift to the grocery store because they tore up a sidewalk last year with their car and you took the car keys away from them. Ahhh—so this is retirement—the land of milk and honey—the nirvana of *Cialis* and wrinkle-free creams. Yep—you bought into Madison Avenue's snake oil rendition of what your retirement would look like. Did you really think you'd be playing shuffleboard on Holland America with gorgeous babes hanging on each arm? Only George Burns could pull that off and look where he is now. Nope; it's more like a dingy with your wife of forty years bailing out water because your obesity has gotten the best of you.

I've got a simple solution to the quagmire you've found yourself in. Forget the Madison Avenue and Hollywood crap about aging and start over. Pretend your space ship just landed in your cul-de-sac next to your Lexus ES 300 and you've removed the purple shroud that's been covering you for sixty years. What do you want to do before that final sunset? I don't know about you but I want to do things I passed up on the way to retirement because I was too timid to take a chance. I've got a buddy who retired from Chevron as a petroleum engineer and has enough hours to triple major in sociology, anthropology, and political science. He soaked up every course at his local community college—courses he didn't have time for on his way to his career in oil and gas. What a gutsy move!

What about the lady across the street who drives a Jimmie with 35-inch rims and wheels big enough to crush a Volvo? She's leading an aerobics class at six in the morning for seniors who haven't found their feet yet. She's sixty-five and looks forty. She runs, she stays out of the sun, she volunteers as editor of her local civic group's newsletter. She makes Cat Woman look like a pussycat. Yes, Dorothy, these people do exist. They've been thinking about retirement for a lifetime and didn't wait until their boss told them they were too old to work.

So what are you waiting for? Jump in. Remember when you looked down from the high dive when you were eight and the water looked like the bottom of the Grand Canyon. That's what fear does—it paralyzes you. It turns grown people into wimps who are too afraid to try something different. Do you want to become another couch potato statistic? One day you get up for another beer and it's over. Your arteries were so clogged with saturated fats that the heart said bye-bye and left you on the floor clutching the TV remote. Your poor wife of forty years had just planned a cruise for the two of you. Oh well; save the tickets for another time and place.

Okay—enough of the grim and morose. Let's take a different track. Begin now to exercise and eat healthy. Reduce the booze and sweets. Get yourself a personal trainer if you can afford one; if not, then walk two miles a day at a brisk pace to get your sweat glands pumping. Join a book club, start writing, volunteer in your community, and help with your local civic organization. Join SCORE (Service Corps of Retired Executives), sign up for some leisure learning classes. If you don't exercise that gray matter between your ears, then plaque and tangles will supplant your nerve endings and you will find yourself smiling at people you don't recognize.

Forget the retirement seminars. They are a waste of time and only make money for those narcissistic motivational speakers who never worked a day in their life. Go with your gut. You know what I'm talking about. That little place inside of you that says—go for it. Who the hell cares what the neighbors may think? Are you still trying to please you family and friends after sixty years? What a boring life. No wonder you're on Prozac. Why don't you "pony up to the plate" and jump into that swimming pool that's been eluding you for sixty years? All it takes is one step. Just put one foot in front of the other and start walking again. The definition of a rut is an open grave and you've been digging one for a lifetime. It's time now to crawl out of that sandy loam and live again.

At the risk of sounding apocryphal, cast a wider net. You'd be surprised what you might pull in if you allow yourself more freedom to explore. Here are some suggestions for those of you who are somewhere between indifference and unconsciousness.

1. Join an exercise class.

2. Take a cooking course.

3. Take a ceramics class.

4. Join a writing group or book club.

5. Volunteer at your local YMCA.

6. Help with a local charity.

7. Read to young children at a local elementary school.

8. Donate your time to improve literacy.

9. Write a newsletter for your civic group.

10. Design your own webpage.

11. Study genealogy.

12. Go on an archeological dig.

13. Get involved with your local alumni chapter.

14. Take up coaching as a second career.

15. Become a soccer referee.

16. Drive the van for a local senior citizen's group.

17. Teach a computer class for seniors.

18. Join a local PC users group.

19. Run for elective office.

20. Volunteer at a local animal shelter.

21. Offer a workshop for seniors on leisure learning.

22. Take a Tai Chi class.

23. Join an RC (radio controlled) club.

24. Take an art class.

25. Volunteer as an usher at your local theatre.

26. Take up ballroom dancing.

27. Write a column for your neighborhood weekly paper.

28. Offer to teach at your local community college.

29. Join AARP.

30. Get involved politically in your local community.

These are just a few suggestions that you've been putting off because you "worked and didn't have the time." Well now you have the time. There are no more excuses. No more creeping or weeping. It's time to get off the pot and shake a leg. In a word—**LEAP**.

L is for learning.
E is for effort.
A is for acceptance.
P is for planning.

Learning: God gave us a brain for a reason and this fact sets us apart from other mammals. If you choose to give up on information after you've graduated high school or college or whatever, then you've wasted your most precious resource. Mental sharpness comes from continued use of your brain. Become an active learner. Forget the remote and sign up for a fun course at your local community college. You might just surprise yourself and develop a passion for learning, perhaps for the first time.

Effort: Effort is trying without weighing the consequences of your decision or attempting to grade yourself. You've been competitive for forty years and now it's time to have some fun. Everything you try from now on is pass/fail, and the only way you fail is to not try.

Acceptance: Accept who you are and quit trying to compare yourself to others. Our society is promulgated on competition—winners and losers. We learn this from preschool and compete until we die if we're so unlucky. It's now time to accept our uniqueness and play down our self-importance. Don't live on past laurels and accomplishments. Treat each day as a new beginning where wonderment and childlike learning can take place.

Planning: Plan for your retirement in your forties. I don't mean financial planning, but emotional planning. Begin to reduce your work week and spend one hour a day learning something new. The game of life is not about living but being alive.

9

Don't Stay Mired or You'll Grow Tired

I had the good fortune to catch Jack (Jake) Klugman's one-man show the other night and he was absolutely amazing. We know him as Oscar in the Odd Couple and Quincy in Quincy, M.D. from his TV shows, but he also starred with Hank Fonda and Lee Cobb in *Twelve Angry Men* along with other movies with Judy Garland, Jack Lemmon, and Ethel Merman. The fact that you may not know is that Jake is a cancer survivor. In 1996 part of his right vocal cord was removed and he lost his voice for six months. Only through painful rehabilitation was he able to learn to speak again, although his voice is softer and more like gravel.

His two-hour show is a testament to a person who refused to quit and feel sorry for himself. He worked tirelessly to recapture is love for stage and theatre; he refuses to live solely from royalties from his TV series and has returned to the stage. He drank slowly from a water bottle as he tells his life story with the help of video clips and photos taken by his son. He takes questions from the audience and with only a hand mike effortlessly and shamelessly tells of his love for the stage and his fellow actors, many of whom are now deceased. His most telling tribute is of his Odd Couple partner, Felix, played by Tony Randall, now deceased.

What does this have to do with retirement? Plenty. Retirement is a myth. It's not an end point or even a transition in someone's life. It's only another turn in the road, and Jake exemplifies how one chooses to travel life's bumpy roads. The Boomers have the advantage of excellent medical care and have kept fit through food and exercise. Many of us will live into our 80s and can look forward to twenty years of celebration or regret. The one poignant comment that Jake's experience teaches all of us is that no one is exempt from life's vagaries. His experience with cancer taught him to enjoy each day as if it's his last. Many of us must suffer a tragedy before we recognize this simple truth, but the lucky ones have already experienced this epiphany.

When you look at older people what do you see? Do you notice gait, appearance, conversation, or their silence? Regrettably, many of us have already given up on life; we trudge through the day watching the clock tick away. Our days and nights are demarcated by TV shows, mealtimes, and phone calls (if we're lucky to receive them). Depression is our enemy if we stay mired in our self-pity and loneliness. No wonder that many visits to physicians by those on Medicare suffer a co-morbid depressive illness. This affects men more so than women because we work alone and retire alone. No wonder suicides for males over 70 are increasing.

There is a better way and we don't have to suffer a life-threatening illness to remind us of the gift of life. A businessman, Ted Cooper, Jr. was pursuing a successful career six years ago. Carefree and agnostic, he soon became mired in a life of sameness; friendships were lacking; he was bored and decided to pick up the bible one day and begin reading twelve pages a day. About halfway through his ninety days of reading the complete bible cover to cover, he became a believer. He quit his job to become founder of "The Bible in 90 Days." Now churches all over the country are introducing this unique concept of small group support, accountability, and discipline to bring meaning to one's life.

I'm not trying to convert anyone to Christianity; but what I want you to take away from the experiences of Jack Klugman (a devout Jew) and Ted Cooper, a born-again Christian, is that life remains a mystery if we don't prepare for the curves and bumps in the road. We need a roadmap and the Koran, Torah, or Bible or other spiritual guidance provides a couple of important insights: (1) we are not alone; (2) people have taken our road before; (3) we can travel alone or with a companion; (4) we don't have to know everything; (5) life is tough and unpredictable; (6) it helps to believe in something greater than ourselves; (7) we live finite lives in an infinite timeframe; (8) someone loves us; (9) it's the dash between our birth date and death date that counts; and (10) we have free will. Let's look at these postulates a little more closely.

We are not alone: The Boomers are the largest cohort of folks approaching retirement (born between 1946 and 1961) when birth rates were high following the end of WWII. We have the advantage of networking with like-minded retirees having been a part of the largest workforce in peacetime to rebuild America after the Second World War. The Eisenhower years were ones of prosperity and hope. The Boomers experienced television, college, drive-in movies, protest, the computer, and terrorism. There have been more changes in the last fifty years than at any other time in our history and this trend will continue as we live faster and more complicated lives. Support groups are important to combat a sense of *anomie* and isolation. There are 12-step programs for every conceivable addiction but none exists for retirement. Why not develop an RA (Retirement Anonymous) group for those of us who are powerless to plan our own retirement?

People have taken this road before: Scott Peck in his book, *The Road Less Traveled,* identified this concept in 1983. We are not alone in the larger scheme of life with generations before us who have dealt with retirement. We do have more leisure time than our ancestors, but the process remains the same—what to do with the time we have left after finishing a career or the children have left home? One can go back to Abraham and Sarah to see the importance of family trials and tribulation and the realization that "life goes on." True, we are born and then we die, but to live life is to develop a passion and meaning that transcends ourselves and our jobs.

We can travel alone or with a companion: Most of us live our first eighteen years as part of a family. Like our ancestors before us life is easier when joys and disappointments are shared. After we leave home to begin our careers we have another choice to live alone or with a help mate. Whether within a traditional marriage or not, sharing space and time builds intimacy and requires discipline and sacrifice. Some of us will spend our retirement years alone after losing a mate, but we don't have to remain alone in spirit or community. There are many senior groups organized around activities mentioned earlier in the book. My advice to those of you thinking about "going it alone" is DON'T. Research shows that living alone is dangerous to your health. Physical and mental illness and suicide rates are higher. You may have retired from a job but not a social network.

We don't have to know everything: Thank goodness we have the Internet to link us to the information highway and chat groups around any interest and endeavor. Instead of driving to the library on a cold, icy morning, we can push a button and click on and tune in. There are support groups for every person from Classmates.com to Veterans groups to cooking classes to our alma maters. There's no excuse for not using the Internet to ward off isolation and loneliness. But remember that the computer is no substitute for joining a group around a common theme and activity. Discussion and interaction are key to staying healthy and hungry for knowledge.

Life is tough and unpredictable: So you didn't make rocket scientist or rock star. You had some bumps along the way like a death, divorce, kid that won't talk to you, a parent who can't remember your name. So? Deal with it! If you've read the autobiographies of famous people you'll soon learn that life is tough. You've heard the adage—when the going gets tough, the tough get out of the way and find an alternative game plan. I've been a firm believer in having a strategic plan for retirement that includes at least three different scenarios: best, worst, and most likely. Write down how you would spend your time and money during the last twenty years of your life with all three scenarios. Chances are that the most likely scenario will be the case although you plan for the best-case scenario. Fortunes have been won and lost; loves come and go; but one thing remains constant and that's your love and respect of self. Don't be shy about spending your time and money on others. It will pay great dividends in ways you've yet to imagine.

It helps to believe in something greater than ourselves: I've alluded to this already with a belief that there is a reason for our being here besides protoplasmic randomness. Purpose is defined not by what we do but who we are. This microcosm called Planet Earth was formed somehow; we may argue science versus creationism but primordial soup requires a chef and a recipe. It is reassuring to know that we are fellow travelers in a life that has a definite beginning and ending. These two points we don't have much control over, but what we do between these end points is up to us. How do you wish to spend your retirement years? It's your life. Take responsibility and decide whether to be an active or passive player in this game of life.

We live finite lives in an infinite timeframe: This is a corollary to the above postulate. Time has value only in the sense that we can measure it; we did not create it nor can we stop it. Our limited existence on this earth may be defined by two end points but the measure of the human experience consists of overlapping points in time. Generations before us experienced life differently than we do; likewise generations to follow will experience life differently. Yet, there are some universal truths that tie these end points together and unite us. Life and death can be the same thing if we stay mired in self-pity and negativity. The more challenging path is to live as if death is knocking on your door. Jack Klugman found this out at age 77 when he was diagnosed with throat cancer. Others experience this when they lose a child. The sad fact is that most of us live as if there's no tomorrow and we consume resources at an alarming rate without regard for our fellow travelers. Self-importance is an illusion predicated on naiveté and selfishness.

Someone loves us: This is important for those in their retirement years. A survey was done a number of years ago in which the elderly described their three most prevalent fears: Number one was not having enough money for retirement; number two was surviving some catastrophic illness; and number three was dying ALONE. Friendships are invaluable. Cancer support groups have prolonged the lives of cancer patients. Companionship is a valued commodity in an impersonal world. Single men die at an alarming disproportionate rate than those in a relationship. For some reason, single women don't because they stay in touch with family and friends. The road less traveled is much easier if we have a companion to walk at least part of the way with us.

It's the dash that counts: Next time you're in a cemetery notice the markers. I'm drawn to the dashes for some reason. Some markers have no dashes; they just have the date of birth and death. Other markers are more artistic and substitute flowers, asterisks, and personal insignia that are recognizable only to family. We have no control over our birth or death (if you discount suicide), but we do control what happens to us in between. Free will gives us the freedom and responsibility to live a life that we define for ourselves. When I attend memorial services for family and friends, I'm amazed that on the front of the program is the beginning and end of one's life, but little mention beyond some basic facts about how a person lived his or her life. That part comes from the participants who came to pay tribute to their friend and family member. Not all comments are platitudes; some are raw, funny, sad, happy, intimate, and personal. Memorial services are not about the dead, but about the living and the impact the deceased had on the lives of those attending the service. Lives touched by our loved ones extend beyond family. I had the privilege to attend the memorial service of a dear friend who died from lung cancer. Not only were his family and friends in attendance but five Vietnamese families numbering fifty people stood up at told the congregation how this person had touched their lives and given their father employment in 1972 and allowed them to invite other family members to the states. Each person was deeply appreciative of this man's time and money given to them and how their lives were forever changed. What a tribute that connections transcend culture, time, and people?

We have free will: This thread is interwoven throughout this chapter. We are the masters of our own fate more than anyone else. We have the choice to remain a victim to the vagaries of life or to embrace life and live it as we want. This sense of omnipotence carries with it a respect for others and to be stewards of the financial and personal resources given to us. The empowerment from understanding that destiny is a process, not an end point changes one's thinking from passive participant to active player. This game of life is not about winning or losing but living in harmony with ourselves and others. Retirement is but another chapter in our lives and how we live it depends on our willingness to take risks and live with its consequences. The decisions we make today may influence our actions for tomorrow, but to think beyond a day burdens the weak of mind and spirit.

10

Retire From What?

Don't believe the crap that financial analysts tell you about having enough money to sit in hot tubs the rest of your lives overlooking a sunset high on *Cialis*. Madison Avenue has such a myopic view of the aging process and seniors are stereotyped as oversexed teenagers with nothing but time on their hands. I don't know about you but I'm sick and tired of being told that I don't have the brains to figure out what to do with my money, time, and relationships.

To listen to the drug companies, there's a pill for every ailment. A right of passage is to have your own pill box to replace your MP3 player. Throw away your Glenn Miller and Tommy Dorsey CDs (the vinyls were tossed in a garage sale long ago). Today you are SENIOR, and PROUD of it. Take that handicapped sticker and display it proudly around your rearview mirror. Claim memory loss when you cut in front of someone in the checkout lane. Load your basket with six gallons of *Blue Bell* ice cream. To hell with the doctors who want you to monitor your cholesterol every six months. And by all means make sure you take your Metamucil. God forbid if your stools are hard as bricks and you become a modern medical miracle during your next bowel movement.

The opposite ads about seniors are just as nauseating. I'm reminded about the ARMY ads, BE ALL YOU CAN BE. We've got former presidents jumping out of airplanes, aging movie stars racing Formulae One cars, 70-year old studs seducing anything that moves, workout facilities in nursing homes (have you ever seen anyone on these machines?) Yes, the "I am Senior" mentality is equally ridiculous suggesting that we need not pay attention to our health and "throw caution to the wind." My favorite commercial is the couple who pretend to have a bad connection on their cell phone as their son is trying to check on them and they're in Vegas dressed to the nines and ready to party. They have this sheepish grin on their face as if they're going to commit some immoral act on the strip.

So the question begs: Retire from what? For those of you who have done little with your life thus far and played it safe, chances are you will notice very little difference when you retire. Your life will continue in its own predictable way: coffee (decaf of course), paper, check your stock portfolio (if you have one), call a few friends over for pinochle, talk to the "grands" and go to Lubys for dinner. For those of you who enjoy intellectual pursuits you will continue to study, read, learn, and challenge your thinking. The old expression "use it or lose it" is true. Remember the anti-drug commercials, "This is your brain—this is your brain on drugs." Well research has shown that the aging brain is the product of genetics, wiring, chemicals, and exercise. The frontal cortex, where learning takes place, continues to light up with bright reds and orange hues on fMRIs in seniors who engage in mental activity. For those who choose a more passive lifestyle, like curling up with the remote control, your brains might register a magenta color somewhere between unconsciousness and awakening.

So here you are. It's the big day. The party was a smash success, complete with balloons, hyperbolic speeches, war stories as you look around at the younger faces, trapped in a Jules Verne, time warp between the world of work and retirement. You're driving home with your mementos in an *Office Depot* file box rattling in the back seat of your gas guzzling SUV, with the radio turned to the "oldie" station. Suddenly it hits you at the next traffic light when this oversized teenager with the boom blasters rattling your windows that you're out of place—kind of like a Republican in Hollywood. Your random thoughts surreptitiously land on the question: What the hell am I going to do now? Your heart begins to beat faster, your hands feel clammy, you have trouble breathing, and you reach for a *Xanax* to quell the panic attack that's about to overtake you and kick this punk's ass next to you. Your mind drifts back to 1952 when you were middle linebacker for your varsity high school team and that zit-faced low-rider pepped up on steroids next to you needs to be taken out. The light turns green and you realize you're back from the Land of Oz, rolling along that familiar road home.

You pull in the drive way of your carefully manicured lawn that you pay $100 a month for the kid next door because your lawnmower didn't pass the emission control test last year. You carry thirty-eight years of work in a 2 x 3 x 2 cardboard box through the front door and sit it down on the coffee table. A note awaits you that your wife of forty years has another date with her personal trainer—Armando. Your college graduate with a degree in sociology is mesmerized by *Cartoon Network*, while eating a bowl of cheerios in front of your plasma TV. Your faithful companion, Brinkley, barely raised his head to acknowledge your presence (Brinkley is also older and requires special dog food for his slower metabolism). You freeze in front of the mirror, looking at a man twice your age in the early stages of obsolescence.

You go to the fridge and remove your favorite beverage, a *Shiner Bock*, pop the cap, and coax Brinkley to join you on the back deck overlooking your sparkling pool that Ernesto keeps clean for $200 a month. The pooch barely raises his head as if to say, *naw, you go cook in the heat, old man.* Sitting next to the spa, you take a long swig from the dark brown bottle while perusing the professionally landscaped "yard of the month," wondering WHAT THE HELL AM I GOING TO DO NOW?

Your thoughts drift back to your first home when you were on all fours plugging grass in the backyard. The wife was putting a new coat of paint on that wooden duplex you rented for $125 a month because you agreed to mow the lawn to save another $25 from your $1000 monthly graduate student stipend. Life was an adventure and you hadn't a care in the world except grading the next exam for your dissertation professor. Yes, this was BK (Before Kids) time, and life was good. Somewhere between BK and SWK (Still With Kids), thirty-eight years of work intervened and changed your life.

BK was a time of sexual enlightenment. When the world slowed down and you and your spouse moved in slow motion across green meadows with the wind at your back. BK was a time of enchantment—when you stared at each other for hours saying nothing, but feeling the warmth exuding from skin yet to be damaged by UV rays. BK was never having to say you're sorry because the pregnancy test came up negative. BK was hanging out with each other oblivious to your surroundings.

But then the not so subtle questions appeared from your parents—when am I going to be a grandparent? It felt like a grenade had landed in the middle of your safe newly painted duplex. A WHAT? A GRANDCHILD? That means getting off the pill; forget about the creams and Trojans. Your job now was to produce another, living human being who would forever change your life and remove all romance from an otherwise perfect marriage. We're talking about the world of KIDS.

A funny thing happened on the way to kids. Remember when free time was the norm? Now you find yourself in the middle of the night half asleep with this infant screaming because s(he) couldn't get enough of your wife's mammary gland four hours before. Now it's your turn and you're scared to death because your plumbing is different and you've never heard of microwaves. You warm the glass bottle of your wife's milk carefully pumped the night before and attempt to insert a round peg into a square hole. Outer space docking in zero gravity was easier than this. The red face in front of you is screaming until your eardrums are about to burst while your wife is nursing a headache (amongst other aches). Finally you get the little booger to open his (her) mouth just long enough to insert the mother ship. Crying ceases and the silence ensues with a big sucking sound (no we're not talking NAFTA). Your precious little one has survived another panic attack about starvation and you can rejoin the world of sleep for another two hours.

A noise awakens you from your daydream. It's your college graduate getting himself another coke from the fridge. His hands are trembling because this is his sixth day of sobriety and the monitoring device around his right ankle registers zero percent alcohol for another small step for mankind. Your thoughts drift back to the KID and how your life changed from stud to eunuch. Your new job was to go find a REAL job now that your dissertation was completed and you had some funny letters after your name that Uncle Joe kept said stood for "post-hole digger."

A face appears. It's your first boss welcoming you to the R&D department of *General Electric*. Your first real job—designing a jet turbine engine that ran on less fuel and produced less noise. Your days were filled with blueprints and schematics. Shop talk replaced "baby talk" as you trudged to work each day with your vinyl-lined pocket with two pens and three mechanical pencils. Black horned-rim glasses and long sideburns stared back at you during your first presentation on "hydrofoil characteristics and its interaction with metal alloys on the leading edge of wing assemblies." The next thing you remember you're giving your farewell speech thirty-eight years later to hip, twenty-some-things with IPODs and laptops.

Somewhere in between computers and slide rulers a mental gap exists that clouds your psyche and renders your brain obsolete from the world of work. Four kids, two grandchildren, three mortgages, a hair transplant, and dental veneers later, you realize that Generation Twelve will make the important decisions that will affect your stock portfolio. The door bangs and your wife of forty years greets you with her "how was your day" speech that *Memorex* would be proud of. Somehow she had forgotten that today was your LAST day of work and life as you know it as a worthwhile, valuable person. Too bad tomorrow wasn't garbage day or you would sit yourself out at curbside.

The wife looks great thanks to her plastic surgeon. Every wrinkle, sag, and excess skin has been judiciously removed like picking out splinters from your fingers. The boobs defy gravity and greet you before she pecks you on the cheek. You look at your roll and love handles and amuse yourself with bariatric surgery, but quickly dispel the myth that you are a walking heart attack ready to explode. You make a mental note to sign up at the gym tomorrow. No more power lunches for you, no Siree Bob; it's carrot juice and *lean cuisine* for the rest of your life.

After finishing your beer you lean back in your easy chair waiting for *Apollo Twelve* to take you into the Netherlands for the remainder of your evening. The wife is busy on the phone lining up a golf tourna-ment for the Ladies Auxiliary; the college graduate has switched from Comedy Central to Grand Theft Auto, his eyes glued to a police cruiser blown to smithereens by an M-50 machine gun in the hands of a 13-year old punk high on crack cocaine. You drift in and out of the world of the living. You find yourself exploring the possibilities of your own demise and how to make it look like an accident. Let's see now—I could say that someone mislabeled the *Tylenol PM* with Potassium Chloride; or spongy brakes are not all that bad; or I didn't realize our pool had a shallow end. No that would be too easy. I'll just sit here a few minutes longer until the wife puts on her C-PAP and call it a night.

Sunlight permeates your eyelids beckoning you to run to the bathroom to relieve your bladder squeezed by an oversized prostate. Somewhere between dark and light you realize that the chair in front of the TV is still occupied. Silence is everywhere. Even Brinkley's snoring didn't awaken you. You stumble upstairs to find your college graduate still glued to the CRT with pinholes for pupils, surrounded by empty coke cans neatly piled in a tribute to the Great Wall of China. Gun shots erupt in surround sound. You cower like a defenseless pawn as another prostitute is run over by a police cruiser. Your son barely acknowledges your existence—this same person who screamed at you every night twenty-four years ago because he was hungry.

You check on your wife and find her on the floor performing her palates to a tape by the bionic woman who looks like *Barbie* and moves like *Batwoman*. You close the door leaving her sweating on the floor. You pour yourself some coffee and sit down with the paper, pretending to go to work today. *I can call in sick. They will miss me and the entire space program will be pushed back ten years.* You realize the futility of your warped ego and return to reading about another drive-by shooting of some poor kid sitting in a car with his girlfriend. After finishing the raisin bran you carefully place your bowl in the sink with the precision of a mechanic replacing the catalytic converter on your SUV. The clock reads 7:05 a.m. By this time you'd be on the 405 fighting every illegal alien for road rights on your way to another place in paradise. You stare at the clock again, the second hand moving ever so slowly to its appointed round with the number twelve. You ponder the question that's been bugging you for a week now: *Retire from what?*

11

No More Work and No More Jerks

Pick up any *Fortune* magazine, *Wall Street Journal,* or business section of your local newspaper to read another article on Bad Bosses. When are folks going to learn that we have absolutely no clue on how to manage people? Peter Drucker, the Man, who regrettably died this past November, 2005, was big on principles, but skeptical on personal qualities needed to manage. Like we need a book to manage our subordinates. This should follow all the other "Dummies" books on parenting, making money, finding your golden parachute, and astutely titled other "how to" books designed to give crappy advice that might make the author money and cure your insomnia.

So what does one do who finds himself or herself on the other side of the chasm from their boss? There are three choices: kiss ass, quit, or develop a coronary. We all know who the ass-kissers are: they're the ones with clean desks who hang out around the copy machine, make all the company events, reply to all emails, and send the boss and his family a Christmas card (if his or her spouse still lives with the boss). My favorite commercial is the poor dweeb who has the punk hair-do and twenty pens sticking out of his pocket protector and choking on his belt who gives a dissertation on the merits of intranet and servers to improve communication within the company. The boss walks by and says "nice job" and continues his course to the plush corner office with the putting green and plasma TV.

Remember when Clinton and Gore were touting the Internet for productivity. Did you know that neither had emailed before Clinton's speech and actually had to be taught how to get online by one of their aides? I'm amazed at the number of ass-kissers who spend each day counting their 401(k) earnings and playing games at work while pretending to write that report that is due on the boss's desk the next morning. There are many steps in the corporate ladder and for everyone above you requiring your undying gratitude there are at least six direct reports below you kissing your ass. No wonder we're stressed by the end of the day—we've been on a merry-go-round of platitudes and puckers.

If you're the John Wayne type and prostrating yourself before your boss creates vision of homophobia, then you can quit. That's it. It's that simple. Just quit. Johnny Paycheck had it right—take this job and shove it. There are many movies and characters that we wish could be more like. The first one was the poor slob in *Network* hanging out the window yelling at the top of his lungs "I can't take this anymore." Or how about Tom Cruise who suddenly takes his lone client has no money to show him in *Jerry McGuire* after finding out he's odd man out. Or the ultimate quit job—*Easy Rider*. Fonda and Hopper had it right, get on that Hog and ride across Arizona with the wind at your back and the empty rode ahead. No more assholes to kiss, no more suits, no more coffee spills, just the open highway and lady luck at your side.

But the vast majority of us poor bastards are too scared to try kissing or quitting. So what happens to us? We fill ERs with chest pains, nervous stomachs, stress seizures, depression, panic attacks, and flatulence. We go to work everyday just like Willie Loman, who sell our souls to the company store just to eek out a living to pay for some new shoes for the wife and send the kids to a community college. We work for thirty years at the same job in the same cubicle for the same smuck who couldn't wipe his ass without a subordinate bringing him the toilet paper. We wonder why we're on Xanax and Lexapro just to punch a clock for eight hours.

And then there's the infamous commute to our low-life cubicle. We fill the freeways with our gas guzzling SUVs with earphones and Mickey D cholesterol and sugar time bombs while we listen to some asshole in a helicopter telling us to take the next exit to avoid an hour delay because some redneck decided to change lanes with his 18-wheeler and take out an overpass in the process. It's Gettysburg in the Burbs. We flip off every driver in the HOV lane with a fake plastic body in the front seat who zips by our poor excuse of a vehicle at ninety miles an hour, seriously hoping that he rear ends a motorcycle cop.

Ahh—the American dream. A job for everyone. Unemployment is down; people are up to their ears in credit card debt; grandparents are parenting our children while the happy working couple spend two hours a day polluting our cities with expensive gasoline with enough additives to make Hiroshima look like a firecracker. And we're supposed to be grateful we have jobs? We consider ourselves lucky to have jobs? Give me a break. This is some horrible mutation of race of human beings stranded on the freeway two hours a day waiting for the next exit to take them to their hell hole for another eight-hour day.

We do have a choice, however. Instead of meeting our medical deductible and keeping every heart surgeon in our country employed, we can say no to freeways, commutes, bosses, and the 8 to 5 grind. And many of us are doing just that. With the advent of laptops, cell phones, Blackberries, Blue Tooths, IPODs, and other electronic paraphernalia, we can now hook up with the 21st century. Instead of IV mainlining shit into our veins, we can plug every orifice in our body with an electronic gadget that does everything but wipe our ass. No more newspapers, stock quotes, soothsayers, pundits, bosses—we can join the ranks of the "plugged in" generation of workers who make money without leaving their "in default" trailer.

That's the ticket. Instead of emulating the 60s generation of tuning out and turning on, we tune in to the information age. There is no boss. The poor bastard has already died from a coronary or has taken his stock options and severance package and living near Roswell, New Mexico, waiting for the next UFO to beam him up. We now work in sweat suits, eating tofu and raisinettes to lower our cholesterol and fight free radicals that might damage our cell life. We trade in the wingtips for the tennis shoes, and tee shirts with no pockets for starched white shirts and pocket protectors. Our coffee pot sits on our kitchen counter instead of some stale cigarette smoke-infested room behind the copy machine. Our cell phone and laptop connect us to any company in the world. Power lunches are replaced by OJ and mouse pads. Health club memberships are replaced by a treadmill in our garage while we listen to Bill Henley tell us the evils of working for an asshole.

So we do have a choice. We no longer have to use lip gloss or suffer coronaries. We join the growing rank of the self-employed. We become empowered to become our own boss—and it's anatomically impossible to kiss your own ass. So now that you've taken the plunge into the world of the self-employed—what do you do? You'd better have a good idea or you will soon find yourself standing in line with your former co-workers for a crummy six-month unemployment check while you skim ads in the paper for hamburger helpers.

With all the hype these days about Covey's books and the magical number seven, I have seven rules for those of you who are considering working for yourselves. This may not necessarily make you effective, but will keep you from becoming inept.

Rule Number One: Stay away from franchises. They will suck up your money faster than an Oreck on a wooden floor. Franchising is a 270 million dollar a year business from operating your own Blockbusters to opening up the next Quiznos on your block. The franchise fees and royalties will drain every penny of profit and leave you working for your real boss—the delirious distributor who sold you that franchise on the promise that you would be your own boss. But alas, if you're one of the unfortunate slobs who just forked over fifty thousand bucks for the right to lease an empty storefront next to an all-night truck stop, then you will find yourself mortgaging your home faster than you can bend over.

Rule Number Two: Stay away from multi-level marketing scams. If it sounds too good to be true, then it is. Plain and simple. Don't go to the free seminars; don't buy the tapes; don't plug into the internet and bulletin boards; don't talk to people who call you by your first name after six o'clock at night. All they want to do is take money out of your pocket and put it in theirs. And that's if you're lucky. A few of us have lost body parts under the guise of working for yourself to establish your own clientele. This is nothing more that the proverbial "pyramid scam" intent on paying off earlier investors with "upfront fees" from later investors. Go to your nearest Attorney General, if one of these assholes gets a hold of your email or phone number.

Rule Number Three: Don't borrow money from family. It's one thing to fail yourself; it's quite another not to be invited ever again at family reunions and holiday events. It's okay if you blew up the nest egg for your son to go to Harvard; it's quite another to see all your nieces and nephews sitting in the same community college classes. You will also be known as "Uncle Almost Made It." You've seen these guys at family gatherings. They're always alone at the food table fingering all the foods before deciding on which one to eat half of and leave the remainder under a party napkin for some poor slob to touch his mouth with. Anyone who tells you that family businesses run smoothly is a liar or doesn't work with his biological family.

Rule Number Four: Never borrow from yourself. You've heard the hype. Some poor idiot has been turned down by five bankers because his business plan looked like it was written by a third-grader on a paper towel. Yet he's able to finance his claim to wealth by taking out a fifty thousand dollar loan on his American Express card. Now he's rolling in the dough and American Express was the only one to see his success. When's the last time you talked to someone from American Express after six o'clock at night? Do these folks sound like financial geniuses? Did they get their MBAs from Wharton? Remember if you borrow money from yourself, then you can't pay yourself until your loan is paid off, typically at eighteen percent interest.

Rule Number Five: Don't go into business for yourself if you can't spell "work." That's right, w-o-r-k. Did you think that some poor underling would bring your coffee to you each morning, call on your customers, do the payroll, sweep your office, and pay your taxes? If you thought so, then you win the "dumb ass" award for entrepreneurs. The reality is you will work harder than you ever had in your entire life for no pay for the first six months. You will do all the crap jobs that others making five figures did while you had the corner office on the sixteenth floor overlooking fountains and caged birds. Too often folks think that working for themselves is easy; if it were that easy, the DJ would look like a straight line going nowhere.

Rule Number Six: Don't be your own boss if you hate yourself. This one's pretty obvious. Forget the previous idiots you worked for when you had your own parking space. You now park on the street because you sixteen year old has his car on four cinder blocks with brake fluid all over the driveway. No more excuses about the SOB who couldn't manage himself out of a paper bag. You ARE the SOB now and it's not about keeping you happy but keeping you in business.

Rule Number Seven: Resist the temptation to hire employees. Forget about growth, expanding inventory, investment capital, taking care of a village of workers. Your allegiance is to yourself. Gone are the handouts and liberal talk about a chicken in every pot. If you hire someone to work for you then YOU become THEIR boss and you're right back where you started from, only this time you are the enemy. Employees will never be happy working for you and their contribution will never pay for their salaries.

12

Don't Quit and Sit

I just returned from *Cinderella Man*, a Ron Howard Production with Russell Crowe as James Bradock and Renee Zeilweiler as his wife. The movie takes place during the depression when then President Hoover's name was associated with Central Park in NYC rather than a dam in Nevada. It's a true story based on Bradock's comeback in his bid to upset Max Baer for the heavyweight title in 1935. Bradock was all but down for the count in life living on public assistance in New Jersey after a promising career gone south because of injuries. This is not another "Rocky Balboa" movie; it's not about comebacks but believing in yourself—that one's life is worth something to fight for. When's the last time you gave up on your job, school, family, friends, God, and most of all—yourself?

Retirement is an illusive term. The mistake we make is treating the word like a noun. It's an ending to a world of productivity. And men especially have equated making money as contributing to family. The "breadwinner" mentality comes from the Depression Era when men stood in "bread lines" for food and work. The fifties popularized the nuclear family as working husband, devoted wife, and adoring children. If you were "out of work" you were a bum. Even Ralph Cramden who enjoyed his job as a bus driver and Ed Norton who worked in NYC's sewers were worthy of providing for family. Take away a man's job and you might as well cut off his arms and legs.

Unemployment was looked upon as a curse in the sixties when jobs were plentiful and anything was possible. We even put a man on the moon—not bad, for a day's work! Welfare was a dirty word, reserved for the lowest of the low. Old men drinking out of brown paper bags epitomized those without jobs. Hoover Town moved from Central Park of the 30s to back alleys in the 60s. Look at the commercials of the 60s: the Marboro Man rode a horse roping cattle; he wasn't playing poker with a cigarette hanging out of mouth. The Gillett Man wanted a close shave for that next promotion; he wasn't going out on a date. Movies also depicted work as man's constitutional right. *The Man in the Gray Flannel Suit* captured the spirit of one man's fight in corporate America. The 80s captured Gordon Gekko's greed in *Wall Street*. This "hunter mentality" continues to this day; only we've traded junk bonds and financial statements for spears and stones.   ·

"No one likes a quitter." Any of you who have played sports as a youngster has had this mantra pounded into your head by an overzealous coach who thought he was Knute Rockne. "Win one for the gipper" made a movie star president where he continued to put a positive spin on winning. More recently Jack Welch's book on *Winning* (2005), a NY Times Bestseller abhors "strategists" in favor of "operations" which is this millennium's playing field of work where companies are described as winners and losers. Work is not for the faint of heart.

This century is indeed the age of technology wherein electronic gadgets will allow us to work smarter. The paradox is that we still are the only western nation who takes less vacation time than Europeans. Japan, India, and China may work our hours at considerably lower wages with the recent outsourcing phenomena. But Americans are losing jobs at a faster rate to foreign human capital than ever before, because our economy can no longer rely on manufacturing to produce jobs.

So why all this fuss about work? Simply put, work drives economies. A capitalist mentality places value on jobs and people to work them. Without jobs we would return to "bread lines" and drain the U.S. Treasury by printing more money to keep up with welfare recipients. Please don't misunderstand—welfare is not a "dirty word." "No jobs" are two dirty words that can quickly transform a booming economy into a recession.

I have a thought. Next time you see someone standing on the corner asking for work, offer them a job. No handouts, just work. For that matter, why not round up everyone on any street corner in America and offer them jobs—if we have to rehabilitate them first, let's do it. In fact, I would propose tax incentives for new hires who haven't worked in the last six months. Or how about letting seniors keep their social security checks while working any number of hours they choose to; by limiting the amount of money retirees can earn becomes a disincentive to work.

So who's been sitting on the sidelines? Is it grandpa who wants to keep his pension and social security? Is it our young people who can't get a job after a four-year college degree? Is it the housewife who returns to college for a degree after her children leave home? Is it the Vietnam vet who can't keep a job because his medication is too expensive? I think I know the answer to this one, and I believe you do, too. *It's corporate greed.*

The corporation has failed their employees. Ask anyone who has worked for Tyco, WorldCom, HealthSouth, or Enron. Where is their pension fund? Where is their reward for showing up everyday at work? The people who have sat on the sidelines during the past decade have been your Boards of Directors. These corporate abuses occurred on their watch and they should be liable. A federal court judge in Texas recently ruled that Enron Directors can be held *personably* liable for damages. This changes the playing field considerably and no wonder CEOs are dropping like flies. And who wants to be a Director for thirty thousand a year when they've already got the golden parachute?

So how do we get out of this hole we've dug for ourselves? I've got a few novel ideas:

1. ERISA plans for everyone in the company with stock options equally available to each employee up to a maximum percentage of their salary.

2. No more than 1000% difference between top management and entry-level employees.

3. All incentives are performance-based.

4. Directors are picked by a vote of top management with at least 25% representative of line managers.

5. No more outsourcing—read my lips, no more outsourcing. That "sucking sound" you heard in the 80s with NAFTA has increased to a vortex of catastrophic proportions as more U.S. jobs are lost to foreign soil.

6. Quit age discrimination; it's illegal and counterproductive.

7. Each new hire has a mentor over fifty for the first year to insure continuity and intergenerational communication.

8. Everyone receives a signature strengths evaluation with performance reviews done annually by one's colleagues. This eliminates the "ass kissers" and "butt kickers."

9. Ten percent of everyone's paycheck goes to a company charity selected by the workforce majority.

10. Retirees are offered incentives to return to the workforce at their choosing.

Let's look at these ideas a little more closely. First, the subject of stock options. Now they're offered primarily to executives who typically have little or no experience with the company and are non-performance based. Have you heard of equal pay for equal work? And what about work value? Is creating a balance sheet any more valuable to the company than driving a truck that delivers packages on time? And while we're at it—how about eliminating hiring bonuses? Let's get away from modeling our corporations like professional sports teams. Our CEOs are not managers. Our "star" (Jack Welch's term in *Winning*) players are not any more important to the company than the poor guy on the loading dock. If you want to stick with the sports analogy, look at baseball attendance since the strike of 1998.

I think it's a disgrace what CEOs make. There I've said it. Call me a socialist or worse, a communist. But I would argue that we take away value from the company when we take *away* opportunities for employees to earn bonuses and stock incentives like the big boys. Pacific Rim countries have much flatter organizations and pay scales than western countries. I would say that our earlier "plantation mentality" of the 1800s has been replaced by a more subtle form of discrimination and that's *reduced earning potential.* How much respect do you have for someone who's earning *ten thousand* times what the mailroom clerk earns? How much teamwork can one infuse in an organization with pay scales that are based on individual merit and value to the company? I think Jack Welch missed the boat on "star players." On my scorecard, they're the "utility players" who can play at multiple positions. I'll take a Craig Biggio any day (he's played second base, center field, left field, and catcher for the *Houston Astros*) over a Roger Clemens.

I don't have to say much else about performance-based salaries after the HP fiasco with Carly Fiorina. She received a twenty million dollar payout by her Board for non-performance. When's the last time you were rewarded for being fired? This unfortunately goes on all the time. This "star CEO" mentality persists today. To think that one person can turn around an organization is ludicrous. Even baseball managers can't perform this magic trick. Look at Phil Jackson's Chicago Bulls—do you think for one minute they won five national titles solely on his *coaching*? Give me a break! Tell that to Scottie Pippen and Michael Jordan. For that matter, tell that to any fan who ever purchased a ticket to attend a Bulls game.

It's time to take the mystery out of selecting Boards of Directors. The "good ole boy" system has never worked; at best, it promotes a myopic view of the organization and at worse, it smells of pork barreling. If you don't have a personal stake in a company then you're not going to be in a position to make the best decisions for that company. It's like asking you to put in sweat equity in a company that you care little about. And how much can a Director learn about a company when they meet only four times a year? Much of their information is filtered by top management who is *being paid* by the Directors. There is no accountability except to self. Accountability should be downward, not upward. Knute Rockne had it right—winning one for the *gipper* is winning one for everyman and everywoman.

Next time you pick up a phone and talk to customer service do you notice the accent? Before you accuse me of racial bias, I plead guilty to bias. I believe in paying a fair wage to those who work and want to support their families regardless of where they live, their ethnicity, and religious preference as long as they are *employees* of the company. Outsourcing is another fancy term for downsizing. It's put software engineers and many other professionals out of work at a time in their careers when they have given many years to their employers. I understand the economics—that it costs more to pay American wages than foreign wages because of our higher standard of living. But if *each* employee were a stockholder in a company, then outsourcing doesn't make sense. Why would you lay off part of your workforce to give larger bonuses to your "star players?"

And here's my favorite—you're too experienced for the position. Heaven forbid that we placed experienced people in our companies. Fire the $80,000 manager and replace him or her with two $40,000 college grads who are wet behind the ears and have no loyalty to the company. Better yet, don't replace your manager, but outsource his job to India. That makes a helluva lot of sense and promotes a sense of fairness to your employees. What kind of message do you think that sends to those middle managers who've worked their butts off for the last twenty years? The fact that they may be obsolescent *is not their fault—it's the company's.* Stop paying lip service to experience if you want to maintain integrity and accountability with your workforce.

Mentoring is an overused word that sounds good but is seldom put into practice. Until wages are determined on work products based on team performance, then mentoring will continue to remain a buzzword without much meaning. My idea is simple. For every new hire, you pair him or her up with a five-year seasoned veteran for their first six months. The apprentice system worked well in the crafts industry in the 1700s and should work well today. If knowledge is power, it should be *shared* to produce even greater returns to the company.

Performance reviews are a joke. They do nothing but CYA for the boss and do nothing to train your workforce. A good twenty percent of a company's operating budget goes to retraining due to turnover (U.S. Dept. of Labor, 2003). Most employees have never received an annual review and those that do have no input into the process. 360 evaluations were a rave the last decade but their negativity did more to discourage employees. When's the last time you were honest with your boss and got promoted?

You want to help our economy? Then give back ten percent to charitable foundations that promote basic human values of fairness, integrity, and sharing through corporate giving. I'm not talking about the golf tournaments and fundraisers that the "big wigs" play in once a year—I'm talking about taking the top ten percent of the company's profit and giving it back to those who cannot help themselves. This lessens the tax burden on all wage earners and takes the government out of handouts for the poor and underserved.

And finally, the reason for this chapter title. Retirees are an underutilized commodity that promotes age discrimination and robs companies of their most valuable resource—seasoned employees who want to stay on in some capacity, whether it's mentoring, teaching, coaching, or sharing knowledge. How one does this (consulting) is less important that what is delivered—and that is knowledge transfer. If we truly want to reward employees regardless of their position, age, sex, or ethnicity, then we must humble ourselves and listen to the wise. Unless we want to reinvent the wheel *ad nauseum*, then we better give credence to those who have gone before us.

13

Today You Are Your Own Boss

In my coaching practice I tell people who are contemplating starting their own business to devote all their time to developing a strategic plan for assessing the probabilities of success or failure in their new business venture. Retirement is no different. Retirement historically implied a passive existence without the ability to become self-employed and earn some income. Sure, you've got the 401(k), Keogh, SEP, SIMPLE, IRA deductions that you can draw down as ordinary income beginning at 59 and a half and mandatory withdrawals beginning at 70 years. But the Boomers will most likely derive supplemental income from consulting, small family businesses, and partnerships through DBAs, LLCs, and S-corporations.

The mindset for starting your own business after sixty is simple: Have fun, work for yourself, stay away from franchises, don't get involved with extended family partnerships, work from home, and don't work more than two days a week. I'd like to expound further on each of the foregoing admonitions.

Rule No 1: Have Fun: This is what life is about, especially after you retire from your "real" job. You've been on the corporate ladder for forty years, got the severance package plus stock options, and now it's time to kick back and enjoy yourself. But after the first two months you will be driving your spouse crazy. Too much togetherness during retirement is not healthy and can lead to marital rifts that you hadn't anticipated. For instance, the wife invites her bridge group over every

Tuesday morning and you're running around in your PJs with your laptop buying and selling on EBay. Or perhaps you're a business or personal coach and you've set up three phone appointments for Tuesday morning. Unless you coordinate with the wife, you might need to rearrange your schedule. (The reverse is true, obviously and the wife could be the coach in this case and the husband might have a Tuesday night poker party).

If you're like most retirees, you've worked for someone else and you may find yourself a little bored and intimated about starting your own business. There are many business coaches who can help you think about the type of business to set up. I've got one client who after retiring wants to return to his first love of photography. In his heyday, he played around with a Nikon EM, a 35-mm SLR. Now we have digital cameras, Photoshop, and printers that eliminate the need for a darkroom and unnecessary office expenses and developing time. All you need is a digital camera, computer, and printer and you're set to go.

Or perhaps you're a gal who just retired from your partnership at a legal firm and you've wanted to open a B&B with your husband in the hill country of Texas. You sell the four thousand square foot home and move northwest of San Antonio and buy a lovely two-story B&B on the Frio River complete with tubing, kayaking, fishing, hiking, and antique shops. The important thing to remember is to "think fun" and not get bogged down with the details of starting a business as a first step. If you do, you will never follow your dream. There's plenty of time later to hire your accountant, business coach, and banker later. Develop a vision that combines your avocation and with a lifestyle that maintains a healthy balance between work and play.

Rule No. 2: Work for Yourself: There's an old saying that the self-employed either can't work or won't work for anyone else. You've spent forty years commuting, lodging, meeting, and delegating with little control over your schedule. You've missed out on the kids' soccer games and dance lessons, time with your spouse, and personal time. It's about time to move that rocking chair into the attic and grab your laptop and pick your brain. Working for yourself is a liberating experience. You don't answer to a boss, don't adhere to someone else's schedule, set your own pace, pick your clients or products, and choose your own hours. What a deal! Who would have thought that you could transform your life from a cubicle to a second career? Granted, joining the ranks of the self-employed can be a little intimating, but there are many business coaches who can help you transform your dream into reality. It's fairly simple to set up a DBA, use a software program like Money or Quickbooks to keep track of expenses, and CPAs to assist with your tax filings. My preference is to go solo but if you insist on working with your spouse or other family member make sure you have a succession plan in place in the event you become incapacitated or move to your ultimate retirement.

The tricks of the trade include first deciding to whether to pay yourself a salary or go contract. My preference is to go contract since you're only working a couple of days a week. If you're working more than that, you've defeated the purpose of your retirement and that's to spend time on activities that cost you little and you don't earn an income. Volunteering, mentoring, leisure learning courses, online courses, new hobbies, and time with family should be foremost in your list of priorities. The next step is to set a schedule of two days a week—e.g. Mondays and Tuesdays, and work from home. If you work virtually with a computer then you have the flexibility to work from anywhere in the world, including vacations. The third step is to network with potential clients who would buy your product or service. Client lists can be bought without scamming if they have indicated that they wish to receive information from you. Good resources are trade associations, other retirees, and people who want to use your service. Finally, devote study time to learn your new business; don't worry about the learning curve. You will improve with each new article, book, contact, and web-based resource tools.

Rule No. 3: Stay Away From Franchises: Fortune 500 had an article this year that graded the top 100 franchises and the caveats and costs of buying into a franchise. With franchising, you work for yourself and it's a full-time job. This defeats rule number one: having fun. A corollary to this rule is to stay away from funding other business ventures. This makes you a passive partner and there's no fun in watching your investment tank without control over the business.

Rule No. 4: Don't Work With Family: The only exception to this rule is working with a spouse, assuming you both want to work together and agree on what you want to do. The B&B concept appeals to many retirees but remember the division of labor is important. If the husband is going to prepare the meals and take care of the maintenance, then the wife may wish to handle the cleaning and recreational activities. I've seen too many hurt feelings, unfair advantage and disadvantage when siblings, cousins, parents and children are employees in daddy's company. Boundaries are diffuse, job descriptions typically are non-existent or poorly defined, pay is unequal, and succession planning is lacking. If you want to spend quality time with your grandchildren and children during your retirement years then stay away from doing business with them. You can't be family and employee at the same time without tempers flaring and drama in the office. I've seen families torn apart, left out of wills, divorces, etc. in family-owned businesses. Remember one person always is the majority shareholder.

Rule No. 5: Work from Home: Why incur the expense of an office when you can work from home? This is a no-brainer. You've commuted your entire career and you deserve the convenience of working from home. Be sure, however, to set up a separate office and keep track of your expenses. Home office deductions are red flags for the IRS, but you can still expense a home office, particularly if it's your only job. My wife and I have separate offices at home, separate computers, but we share a printer, fax, and phone line for Internet use. I've got a coaching practice while my wife develops lesson plans for early childhood programs. Working only two days a week from home (I would suggest that you and your wife pick the same days, if possible, if you want to spend more time together).

Rule No. 6: Two is the Number: If you're working more than two days a week, then you're defeating the whole purpose of enjoying your retirement. Keeping track of a business takes work and time and sixteen hours a week is plenty to keep the creative juices flowing without becoming bogged down in details. If you find yourself turning down invitations to go out with family and friends or putting off vacations, then you haven't retired. You've just left your cubicle of forty years and substituted your cubicle at home.

I hope I've given you food for thought in how to balance work and retirement, if you decide you want to derive a secondary income in addition to your investments. The money derived from working at home is secondary to the enjoyment of staying active and learning new things. Your mind will remain sharp and you have the ability to mentor and share your knowledge gained over many years. For those of you eager to embark on new paths, the excitement of learning a new vocation without much financial risk can only occur if you're not bogged down in a career. Retirement offers an excellent opportunity to explore new knowledge, skills, and abilities.

14

Stay in the Past and You Won't Last

You've seen the grandparents proudly displaying pictures of the grand-kids and the trips to the Bahamas on the desk that's only used as a cen-terpiece for the family's visual history. I think this is great, but why can't the same table be used for a late night rendezvous or poker game? I 'm always suspect when all anyone over seventy can talk about is their grandkids. Hey—get a life! Let the kids and grandkids have a life and don't be a doting grandparent who lives vicariously through their fam-ily tree.

There's plenty for seniors to do with their own kind. Cruises, trips, dude ranching, biking, hiking, sightseeing, archeology, book clubs, not to mention the endless card and board games. I'm not talking about shuffle board and pinochle; nope; Cranium, Fact or Crap, Travel Plan-ner; Balderdash; games that are funny and get the brain synapses hum-min' while you play for dough.

Down here in Texas I'm amazed at the number of tour buses that leave the senior retirement communities and head straight for the Loui-siana border for a night of gambling. Old grandmas on oxygen pushing quarters into a slot machine faster than a speeding bullet, a cigarette dangling between their varicose veins in their other hand. These are the same "blue hairs" who were on a respirator just a month ago gasping for their last breath, only to be revived to smoke another day. I don't think the Boomers want to spend their retirement watching for three apples or sevens to come up.

It's a proven fact that to live in the present is to maintain a healthy respect for aging and the limitless possibilities for personal growth and enjoyment. War stories are for those who hate the present and have no future. Card tables and dominoes are fine for those too obese to move without an oxygen tank draped over their shoulder. While I can sympathize for those who find themselves physically impaired, most of our ailments are the result of self-inflicted carcinogens and poor nutrition. No wonder that obesity is the number one public health problem in America today.

Our body chemistry is such that metabolism slows down with age and weight gain becomes an insidious harbinger of Type II diabetes, sleep apnea, hypertension, arthritis, and assorted chronic fatigue symptoms. Exercise is important to remain healthy and to prevent the onset of age-related disease. The body is a remarkable vessel and should be treated with respect. Heart disease is directly related to the girth around one's abdomen in men and arthritis and bone density is compromised by obesity. So slow down on the late night snacks and garbage we ingest because we're too lazy to read labels.

I've placed two family members in nursing homes and it's not a pretty sight. My godmother was recuperating from a hip operation and was placed in a nursing home for a month during her recuperation. The nightly sounds in a nursing home would make Freddie Krueger run for his life. It's not for the weak of heart or mind. Men huddled over their urine-soaked wheelchairs tied by wristbands to keep them from falling out. Ladies shuffling down the hall for the next ice cream social half-dressed. Over-burdened nursing staff with limitless charting to justify their jobs and deception of caring for your mother or father. If you can avoid placing a loved one in a nursing home even for one day, I highly recommend alternative care, assisted living, or community retirement homes no larger than 16 beds.

Modern medicine is capable of prolonging life but quality depends on preventative health choices made in your forties and fifties. Just because you're not as agile and quick doesn't mean you can't exercise. One of the best decisions you can make is to hire a personal trainer and follow a nutritious diet high in fiber, low in carbs and sugars, with no more than a glass of wine daily if you must drink alcohol. When's the last time you were in a 24-hour fitness facility? If it's been more than three months, then that's too long. Most of the people today are either young mothers who have just had babies or retired seniors looking to stay fit. It's remarkable that I don't see more thirty-somethings at my workouts.

Some of my suggestions for staying fit include, but are not limited to the following lifestyle changes:

1. Eat three balanced meals daily; don't skip and don't eat after nine in the evening; the body tends to store up fat overnight.

2. Hire a personal trainer at least for the first month and get on a regular exercise regimen. You will feel better and have more energy at night.

3. Engage in intellectual activities that keep your brain active; reading and board games are fun ways to keep the synapses firing.

4. Control your anger; the number one cause of heart attacks is uncontrollable anger; next time you feel like flippin' off that zit-faced teen who just cut in front of you on the highway, think twice; you could be one step closer to your last breath.

5. Keep a joke book or humorous view about life; learn to laugh at yourself; you'd be surprised at how many active seniors laugh at themselves; it's a cultivated skill and easily learned if you don't take yourself too seriously.

6. Keep a journal and write your thoughts and feelings for later reading and review. We can change bad habits only if we keep track of our mistakes and past indulgences. When we are having a "bad hair" day, write about that, too.

7. Pick up the phone (or cell phone) or email a friend at least weekly. Socialization is important in fighting depression and a sense of loneliness.

8. If you have Internet access, join a chat group of retired seniors to share information about trips and activities. A caveat, though—never share personal information that might identify you and be aware of scams on seniors. Don't ever give out social security numbers or credit card numbers unless you have initiated an on-line purchase and you are on an https encrypted site.

9. Join a cooking class or wine-tasting group; culinary pursuits are important to your palate and mental health.

10. Join a same-sexed friend for breakfast at least twice monthly to maintain an emotional commitment outside your immediate family.

11. Develop a spiritual connection with a community of believers who believe in miracles and marvel still about our beautiful world.

12. Maintain an active prayer life and personal relationship with God.

13. Maintain a healthy skepticism (rather than cynicism) about strangers who appear overly friendly. Seniors are unsuspecting targets of financial scams.

14. Live each day as if it's your last; do something for yourself and at least one other person daily.

15. See your doctor regularly and seek second opinions on any recommended surgical procedure.

16. Get into therapy or coaching if you need help with a problem or want an accountability partner to keep you on the right path.

17. Stay in touch with family at least weekly and plan one extended family vacation annually. However, maintain boundaries and do not become enmeshed with your children and grandchildren.

18. Do not spend more than three hours daily on the computer. I realize that web access is great for information and entertainment; but the computer is no substitute for writing a letter, a phone call, or personal visit.

19. If you're in a relationship, set aside one night weekly for a date. Pretend this is a first date and you want to learn something new about your partner.

20. Get at least eight hours of sleep each night. Our bodies and mind need to recharge from the day's activities if we're to remain active and healthy.

Now I know many of you think that this is no more than grandma's advice and you're right to a large extent. These common-sense prescriptions for living a healthier life have been passed down by generations but we now have modern medicine to prolong life if we take care of our bodies and mind. Many of our chronic diseases are self-induced by ingestion of particulates and substances harmful to healthy tissue and organ regeneration. We have a responsibility to care for ourselves. Moderation and patience is the key to a longer life.

So the choice is yours. Do you want to stay mired in the past and reminisce about the "good ole" days? Or do you want to work yourself to the bone to "save for a rainy day?" Past and future are excuses for not taking responsibility for ourselves in the present. Next time you're at the mall, pick out the healthy seniors and understand what sets them apart from their colleagues who don't look as healthy. I would bet that the above twenty rules were observed more often by those Boomers who choose to live in the present and have a smile on their face.

15

You Talkin' To Me?

A great line by DeNiro in one of his many gangster' movies is apropos to this next chapter. Another movie line is when Kathy Bates bumps the younger chicks' car out of the way for a parking space and says "that's okay, I've got more insurance than you." Seniors are getting tougher—no more wimping out on oatmeal and dentures. It's time for Tai Chi, Yoga class, the Y, your personal trainer, Giorgio, and the tanning salon. I just watched a movie, *In My Shoes*, with Cameron Diaz and Shirley MacLaine as her grandmother who's taking care of her fellow seniors at the local retirement home in Miami. No getting down and feeling sorry for herself since her husband died in this movie; no siree, the grandmother is running the place like Patton's Third Armor Division. Remember when seniors were relegated to sitting on the sofa knitting or playing canasta? That may have been your grandmother, but it's not for the Boomer.

Many changes have taken place since 1946, not the least of which has been the advent of the computer and information age. The last computer class I attended was ninety percent seniors who were learning the ins and outs of the Internet and email so they could stay in touch with their grandchildren, children, and friends. Now seniors are buying digital cameras, IPODs, and MP3s to listen to their latest music, email pictures, and catch up on the latest news. Don't worry about the cataracts. Newspaper print is overrated and the news reads like a CSI series.

Today's senior is hip, handy, happy, healthy, hearty, and humorous. Let's take a look at why.

Hip: Throw away the white-buckle and suede shoes; today's seniors sport Reeboks, Nike, New Balance, and other walking shoes that define a lifestyle in the fast lane. No couch potatoes here; it's mall walkin' time, Senior Olympics, marathons, swim meets, triathlons. Grandma and grandpa have replaced the Grand Marquis and Crown Victoria with an SUV to haul the grandkids around to their soccer games, band practice, and voice lessons. While ma and pa work to keep up with inflation the kids keep the grandparents busy and active. It's not unusual for the school to have cell phone numbers for grandma and grandpa who can rush to the school quickly to retrieve a disruptive kid or attend an awards ceremony. We Boomers know the lingo; we after all were the first generation to openly question authority during the Vietnam War. We were the first to break the "glass ceiling" for women in executive positions and Title IX allowing women sports in colleges and universities. Now the boyfriends are going to the girls' sporting events; no more carrying your girlfriend's books; she's got a 50-pound backpack that she sports around like a feather.

Handy: When's the last time you asked your parents to help you with a science project, sew a button, or change out the garbage disposal? Don't be surprised if you got call waiting and placed on hold while mom and dad close on that important deal. Thank goodness we have Boomers who grew up with "Mister Wizard" and the "Maytag Repairman." Granddad is in the garage surrounded by his power tools, wood, and saws, creating mahogany tables and furnishing extended family households. Thanks to modern medicine we're not inflicted with carpal tunnel or arthritis to the point that we can no longer use our hands. And who is going to cook from scratch for that holiday dinner? I don't think it's Generation XY. Nope—grandpa's favorite store is Home

Depot rather than the bait and tackle shop. Seniors are renovating their homes and turning those spare bedrooms into media centers, game rooms, and libraries.

Happy: Seniors today have more disposable income and have invested wisely for the most part. Instead of moving into a Del Webb retirement community, they've chosen to buy a "fixer upper" in the country, buy some cows, and chop their own wood. Ronald Reagan galloping on his horse and chopping wood on his ranch at the young age of 70 was the image that AARP wanted to portray to seniors. In the year 2020, more than one-fifth of our population will be over 65 and we will not be part of the "Prozac" generation. With more discretionary income we will experience more from life than any previous generation because we are living longer and staying healthier. Happiness begins at home and remaining independent after the kids have left propels seniors to new heights and states of awareness. Long-distance learning and leisure learning classes are popping up everywhere and today's seniors are learning junkies who grew up with Sputnik and the Space Race. Look for more seniors to return to college to audit courses and take up second and third careers.

Healthy: Modern medicine has extended our time on earth to 78 for men and 82 for women in this 21st century. The fastest growing population is the 85 plus group. Living longer provides increased challenges and opportunities for retirees. We're now in uncharted waters when it comes to living arrangements, income sharing, estate planning, and redefining extended family. We now have grandparents raising their grandchildren due to increasing divorce rates and single moms having to work. Generation XY is not saving for the future—in fact their net worth is on the negative side with increasing credit card debt and no retirement contributions. The Boomers may be the last generation to experience health benefits that will emphasize preventive care and healthier lifestyles. Hospital stays are reduced and funeral homes are looking for additional income because many Boomers prefer cremation to burial. DNRs, living wills, and durable power of attorney for health matters are common lingo now. Retirees are not content to sit in a rocking chair staring death in the face; instead, they remain productive and provide many volunteer hours and community service.

Hearty: Our pioneer ancestors were a hearty bunch, crossing lonely and hostile prairies on their move westward until the ripe old age of 47 when tuberculosis or malaria killed them. Nutrition and health define today's lifestyle with seniors counting carbs and calories, grams of fat, and cholesterol. Doctor's offices are filled with Medicare recipients who continue to fight to stay healthy and fit. Retirees exercise more today than any generation before. Go to the park or mall and watch the seniors with their New Balance sneakers turning corners and heads. Grandpa and grandma now have personal trainers who keep track of body mass index, fat burns, and aerobic heart rates. My job allows me to frequent my local Ballys during mid mornings and the place looks like a senior citizen center on steroids. Sweats have replaced sweets and aerobic classes have replaced solitary workouts.

Humorous: Archie and Edith Bunker define our parent's generation as they aged and became more reclusive and cynical. Negative thinking and depression are partners in a terrible twist of fate that leaves many seniors immobilized by fear after retirement because they saw their parents before them work until they died. We are now faced with twenty years of "retirement." This can be our wilderness experience or an exhilarating opportunity to experience life free of the encumbrances of children, job, and responsibility. For workaholics this is scary stuff, but it doesn't have to be. Research has shown that laughter is oftentimes the best medicine to combat apathy and depression. A diet rich in comedy may just prolong and enrich one's life. Don't allow your world to close in on you; although we all lend up in a box or urn, it's the DASH that gives life excitement and purpose. Take yourself too seriously and you will suffer many disappointments; take yourself lightly and you will be pleasantly surprised that the load is easier and more manageable. Learn to laugh at yourself and the vagaries of life. To laugh is to live—to cry is to die.

So back to DeNiro. The next time some young punk with zits looks at you like an alien, square your shoulders and look him straight in the eye and deliver DeNiro's line. This old man no longer rocks on the porch and the old woman no longer lives in a shoe.

16

Hey Punk You Feel Lucky?

You've seen the movie. The bad guy stares up at the barrel of a .44 magnum, "the deadliest weapon known to man," in the clenched hand of none other than "Dirty Harry." I love Clint Eastwood. Besides being an accomplished musician (did you know he wrote the score for *Midnight of the Garden of Good and Evil?*) and artist, he is a helluva director and actor. Dirty Harry was my kind of guy—an aging cop with no place to go but down. He was on the other side of work, edging his way to a grave or retirement. That's how it should be, shouldn't it? The choice is ours; we can live our last years in an open grave (aka rut) or retire.

As I had my morning coffee today at Starbucks I happened upon a table of old codgers sippin' on Java and spinnin' yarns of the "good ole days." White hair or no hair, it doesn't make any difference. These dudes were having a blast; no clock to punch; no numbers to crunch; and no business lunch.

The "fast track" is a myth we buy into because we're naïve and greedy. B-schools spew this crap about MBAs and PhDs as one's ticket to the corner office overlooking the peons huddled under bridges. Why do we fear success or failure? We spend a lifetime bustin' our asses to stay one step ahead of the tax man, ex-spouse, or no-count kids who refuse to work and want a free handout. Is this how you spent your work years? If so, count yourself as the majority of us poor slobs who crawl out of a warm sack, crank up the Beemer with sixty payments left, and hunt for that lone parking space four stories underground. We do this until some zit-faced punk who's your boss tells you that your services have been outsourced to someone who doesn't speak English in a country you've never heard of before.

Your pictures of the wife and kids are thrown into a cardboard box by the dude who sports a security badge on his blue jacket and you're escorted back to your underground dungeon for your trip home. You push Don Henley into the changer below your dashboard and listen to "Dirty Laundry" after flippin' off the security guard as you drive out the parking garage for the last time. It's ten in the morning and you stop at a local convenience store, pull a four-pack of Chardonnay off the rack and begin to crack the tops as you guzzle down the clear liquid that refreshes. You Hawaiian salute the flags in front of your sixty-story office building overlooking Lake Michigan as you take the southerly route home to the "burbs."

You open your front door of your overly priced patio home to find your wife on the Elliptical while she cruises to Elton John with the MP3 player strapped to her sinewy arm that looks like an Arnold lookalike. She doesn't acknowledge your entry as you plop down on the leather sofa and hit the remote and find Opie and Andy heading to the lake with fishing poles over their shoulders. You crack open the last Chardonnay while you contemplate how you're going to make the next house payment and keep your Beemer from getting hauled away in dead of night.

The wife asks why you're home so early. Your facial expression says it all. She sees the cardboard box on the floor and instantly realizes she's married to a loser whose only excuse is his age. She begins to rant and rave about how right her mother was for marrying you while you gulp down the last Chardonnay and look for the rubbing alcohol to ease your pain. An argument ensues and the last thing you remember is the smell of burning rubber as the Beemer knocks down the mailbox on your way to the nearest liquor store for a little R&R. The owner barely speaks English but he immediately recognizes you and hands you a bottle of Jack.

The next thing you remember is waking up in a jail cell with a stench strong enough to kill the Avian Flu. The sound of a key brings you back to reality. Your next-door neighbor has paid the bail bondsman his bounty to save your ass from gaining a new orifice. You crash on your buddy's couch to the sound of Infomercials on how to win big in Vegas at Texas Hold-em tournaments. The next image you see is a burst of sunlight as the blinds beckon a new day to remind you that you have no job to go to.

A glass of OJ and bottle of Tylenol await your next move. A note from your wife informs you that she's filed for divorce with an attorney who owes nothing on his Beemer. You drag your sixty-year old body to a shower to remove the forty years of sweat and heart palpitations spent working your ass off to make your boss look good and the stockholders happy. The sweet smell of lavender Olay and warm water cleanse your pores reeking of alcohol. You look in the mirror while drying off to notice the crow's feet and hair growing out of your ears and nose. The once flat belly is now a paunch deserving of a Budweiser commercial. What happened to the athletic MBA from Harvard who exuded piss and vinegar thirty years ago?

◆   ◆   ◆

You wake up from your nightmare to your alarm reminding you of another glorious day of retirement. The sunshine peeping through the wooden blinds portend another round of golf in the Arizona desert. The wife walks in barely breathing after her three-mile run at five thousand feet sea level. She jumps in the shower and then dishes up a quick omelet, toast, and coffee. The two of you jump in your golf cart, hit the garage door opener, and mosey down the driveway thirty yards to the number one tee. You spend the next three hours following a white ball fifty-two hundred yards through the most beautiful red mountains you've ever seen. You stop at the clubhouse for a game of bridge with your friends who just moved from Chicago. The rest of the afternoon is spent placing calls to your kids who are neatly secured in some high-rise office building while trying to make their next house payment. You grin after you punch the "end" key and finally realize that you've made it.

The wife has tickets to the opera that evening after dining in on chicken Caesar salad and Chardonnay. The center aisle seats allow you to experience the drama and music without the distraction of the digital readout of the English lyrics. After the play you park your Acura MDX next to your golf cart in the garage and return to your patio home for a night cap overlooking a full moon against an Arizona sky, with silhouettes of jagged rocks protruding towards the milky sky. The air cuts through your lungs with a smell of Jasmine as the prairie animals make their way across the cool ground for a nightly morsel of peanuts. You lean back in your wrought-iron cushioned chair sippin' on a Tawny Port to cleanse the palate of salt. A warm flow of liquid rushes towards your stomach like a baby's sucking of warm milk to ease the tension of the day.

You look across the table at the woman who's been your true companion for thirty years and admire her strength and beauty. The moonlight outlines her youthful jaw and chin while her blue eyes reflect the creamy light back towards you. You squeeze her hand in silence except for the breeze cutting through the Sega Palms bordering your patio just outside the burnt orange stucco. The late hour signals an intimacy to be shared by two who know each other all too well. A night of lovemaking closes another chapter in this life of retirement for two people who had a vision thirty years ago. This morning's nightmare now seems light years away.

17

Do I Look Retired?

You've seen the bumper sticker "I'm spending my grandchildren's inheritance." This may sound selfish, but the message is not so subtle: people are not content to sit around and wait to die. Hopefully, sound financial advice has given retirees a number of avenues to leave part of their wealth to their children and grandchildren. Any financial planner can walk one through annuities, gifts, trusts, and life insurance policies to bequeath to our heirs. Many of us will not have a need for such financial instruments because our estates will be below the $2 million per person in the year 2006 to escape "death taxes" in which we will not have to give to Uncle Sam dollar for dollar what we have saved for our children. Any estate lawyer can attest that large estates can be exempt from estate taxes with revocable and irrevocable trusts in which our assets are placed in trusts with designated beneficiaries and the tax burden transfers to our heirs who hopefully are taxed at a lower income.

The Boomers grew out of the "me" generation in which our parents doted on us and gave us everything we wanted. Our parents went through the depression of the early thirties and are well acquainted with poverty and "making ends meet." Bread lines and boarders were a reality to help a family survive harsh economic hardships. As a result, our parents became a generation of "savers." The majority of us who grew up as part of the middle class were lucky to go on one family vacation a year. Holiday Inns were extravagant and the family car was the major mode of transportation. Today we have kids flying to the Caribbean for

Spring Break. College students spend an average of six years today to attain a baccalaureate degree with time off to study in Europe. College loans are a booming business for Sallie Mae and families take out parent loans to send their children to public universities.

The "professional student" becomes an asset to a university who is not held accountable for the exorbitant tuition increases that exceed the consumer price index. Furthermore, colleges "sell" a degree without any assurance that the student can land a job upon graduation. A four-year degree today barely qualifies one for a thirty thousand dollar entry-level position and students today must pursue professional advanced degrees in medicine, the law, business, or other graduate programs to at least qualify for more technical positions in government and the private sector.

So what does this have to do with retirees? Plenty. Mom and dad will be working to fund educational programs for their children and grandchildren. Parents are going back to school after their kids land a job or finish high school to improve their learning potential and to keep up with the informational demands of technology and innovation in the workplace. In the late 1800s when many of our land grant colleges were funded, a liberal arts education was the *sine qua non* of elite opportunities for entry into business and industry. I was fortunate enough to attend two state universities when tuition was $50 an hour and a work-study program is all one needed to fund their college education. Now the majority of students and their parents are in debt to Sallie Mae for ten years at interest rates exceeding six percent. No wonder many students are defaulting on their loans because they can't find a job to pay their educational debts much less rent, utilities, and a car payment.

Have you stopped to consider how many older people are still working after sixty five? For some it's an opportunity to get out and meet people but for the majority we've taken out second mortgages on our homes to fund educational programs for our children and grandchildren. For other wannabe retirees we've opened our homes to an increasing number of our children (and their babies) because of unwed pregnancies and divorces. So throw away your hat that says "retired" on the bill because the Boomers will be working well into their seventies.

What are some of the pitfalls that we've encountered along the way to retirement? I'll mention a few, but the reader will undoubtedly think of more.

Consumerism: We've become a nation of consumers. We spend money we don't have. For the first time in 2006, people are spending more than they're earning. Forget savings. We are going into debt! The reasons are subtle but pronounced. We've been duped into believing that we can "buy now and pay later." Credit is easy to attain as witnessed by the avalanche of credit card offers for our children who are approaching eighteen. We can refinance just about anything under the illusion that transferring principal to a credit card with less interest somehow eliminates debt. Paying minimums does nothing but make more money for credit card companies who rely on our greed and stupidity.

Aggressive marketing: We are deluged with ads that define our identity by the labels we wear, the gadgets we buy, and the cars we drive. More is better as evidenced by the bumper sticker "he or she who has the most toys wins." Ever see a personalized license tag on a Ford Escort? The Beemer generation has become "entitled" and believes that they've "earned" a better car, house, and computer, whatever. Madison Avenue spends billions of dollars convincing us that we deserve better, even if we can't afford it. Credit and counseling used to be two different professions but now they're uniquely intertwined to help bail out families who have extended themselves into the next century. It should be no surprise that the largest segment of our society declaring bankruptcy today are seniors who find themselves maxed out to keep up with soaring medical costs, not to mention taking care of their children and grandchildren.

Elitism: Pride is one of our seven deadly sins if one cares to read the Bible. It used to be that "keeping up with the Joneses" was reason enough to consume more stuff. Now we must make a "personal statement" to the world that we are better than our neighbor as evidenced by larger homes, gas-guzzling SUVs, biggie-sized fries and sodas, enough sports equipment for our children to fund a major league ball team, tennis, soccer, drill team, music, (fill in the blank) lessons and camps to merit a second income to feed our children the myth that more is better. Americans are working longer than their European counterparts; chronic diseases and obesity are public health problems of national significance. We talk about RAM, megabytes, and megahertz as a holy grail. Yet with all the technological advances our younger generation are socially inept, ill-prepared for job stress, and lack common sense on the questions that really matter—family, personal growth, spiritual awareness, and egalitarian compromise that does not subscribe to a "zero-sums" mentality.

Financial servitude: Before the industrial revolution and the growth of unions we "bartered" for goods. It was not unusual for the local doctor after making a house call to take home a chicken for his evening meal. Look at any major skyline in the U.S. today and you will find buildings owned primarily by financial institutions and insurance companies. Where do you think they get their money? They don't print it, so we, the consumer, must be contributing to their bottom line. Remember the old Tennessee Ernie Ford song "Sixteen Tons, another day older and deeper in debt; I owe my soul to the company store." Have you seen the bumper sticker "I owe, I owe, it's off to work I go?" Or I love the commercial about the guy washing his two cars in front of his beautiful, oversized home say "how can I afford all this—why I'm up to my eyeballs in debt." And our nation is not at all setting an example as we go into trillion dollar debt and social security becomes an oxymoron.

A scenario: The Cleaver family has been replaced by the Sopranos and Desperate Housewives. Greed, corruption, infidelity, murder, sex, violence, and money have replaced old-fashioned American values of the forties and fifties when we "worked for an honest day's pay and our word was our bond." William Bennett's prophetic admonition, *Book of Virtues*," bemoans the fact that we've turned away from core values and beliefs that this country was founded, and have morphed into a nation of consumers, hell bent to spend every last nickel on consumer products that don't necessarily make one's life better. The "good neighbor" rule as been replaced by "outwit and outspend one's neighbor" and sell the deception of the "good life." This gloom and doom scenario while apocalyptic in tone, nevertheless, captures the reality of unchecked spending. Our children's children will ultimately pay the price with a depression that this country hasn't seen in a hundred years.

So grab your "gimme" caps, Boomers, but be prepared to draw a circle around the word, "retirement," and draw a line through the circle. The fact remains that until we transform our society from a nation of spenders to savers, we will most likely work until we drop dead. For those of you who are sitting in airports with your laptops, cell phones, and IPODs, you will keep yourself busy enough so as not to address this existential question of uncontrolled spending. *Carpe Diem.*

18

Step Aside and Let Me Thrive

Seniors are sold a myth that they are no longer useful once retired. Our national media portrays older people as fools, charlatans, senile, and useless. I just finished watching the movie *Failure To Launch*, with Sarah Jessica Parker and Matt McConaughey. It's a simple enough premise that older single adults in their twenties and thirties continue to live with their parents who feel trapped in a time warp until little Johnnie or Susie decides to leave the nest. The movie's main hero and his two buddies (who also live at home) try to convince Tripp that he should not fall for the temptress played by Sarah Jessica Parker because love will lead to flying the coop—never mind that mom (played by Kathy Bates) and dad (played by Terry Bradshaw) are portrayed as overgrown teenagers without the zits. Bradshaw's nude scenes were disgusting and added nothing to the story except to stereotype older folk as idiots.

It's no wonder that Hollywood's biggest audiences are prepubescent teens who are suspended in a moronic world for two hours while brain synapses lay dormant. Any semblance to a reality is sophistry under the guise of "entertainment." Seniors must look to other media outlets for more accurate portrayals—independent films, cable TV, nonfiction documentaries, etc. What's holding seniors back from continuing to thrive and grow spiritually, emotionally, and intellectually? The answer simply is "stereotypes." To stereotype is to simplify and denigrate. I would suggest a long list of adjectives that break the adolescent stereotypes of seniors in the Western World.

Hardiness: If you've made it to sixty it's due to more than just good luck. You must be doing something right or you wouldn't have sent the "failure to launch" kids to college, looked after grandma and grandpa, while holding down two jobs and running for city council. Today's Boomers may have been slackers in their twenties but the VW Bus has been replaced by the Volvo and the kids in their thirties must like something about living at home with mom and dad besides the free rent. We've been through Vietnam, Grenada, Afghanistan, Desert Storm, the death of a president and his brother, a civil rights leader, the resignation of an American president, and countless economic disasters beginning with the first oil embargo of 1972. We may not be from the Depression Era, but we've landed our fifth job in thirty years because of obsolescence, outsourcing, disloyalty, and greed by America corporations. I would say we're *survivors* and stamina must count for something.

Innovative: The computer generation belongs to the Boomers. We've experienced the rocket launch of the personal computer and the constant upgrades over the past twenty-five years in bringing megabytes of information into our homes and offices. The ability to think outside the box has given seniors opportunities unknown to our parents and grandparents. We've adapted to constant change. More seniors today are signing up for computer classes than any other age group. Seniors are starting home businesses, taking consultant jobs, mentoring, volunteering, and innovating than ever before. Witness the number of small businesses popping up all over the country. *Fortune Small Business* is now a magazine attuned to this phenomena and the largest economic growth is in small business.

Flexibility: Anyone who can handle five different jobs in their career is talented. The Greatest Generation worked for the same company for thirty years, got the gold watch, and retired to a golf course in Florida. Now we have Boomers who were once architects, designing golf courses. As outsourcing becomes more common amongst our American corporations those in their fifties are taking early retirement and starting their own companies. Seniors are banding together and buying homes instead of moving into "retirement villas." The next wave of housing for seniors will be downtown lofts convenient to shopping, restaurants, and entertainment, thereby reducing the need for a vehicle at increasing fuel prices.

Boundless: With the advances of modern medicine in prosthetics, nutrition, and exercise energy levels continue well into our sixties. Ever been to a ski resort in the summer and notice the number of seniors hiking and walking the trails once traversed by snowboards and skies? With hormonal and other endocrinal advances women no longer have to quit living at menopause. Men are not relegated to rocking chairs after knee or hip replacement surgery. Extreme sports while relegated to the young are but a fragment of the total vacation and resort industry built around Boomers with money. Go on a *Holland America* cruise and notice the number of seniors swimming, exercising, and dancing. Have you noticed that the main deck chairs are empty for the most part? The formal sit-down dinners are slowly giving way to ethnic, fast-food, and sushi bars for those seniors who cruise to gain knowledge, muscle tone, and friendships, rather than pounds.

Called: We spend the first half of our lives in a profession that for most of us was serendipitous. As we immerce ourselves in the world of the spiritual, a new word begins to describe who we are and where we're going. In our past life the word, "driven" might have captured this theme, but *driven* is externally motivated by negative consequences whereas a *calling* is internally motivated to a higher power outside ourselves. Callings can grip people at any age, but we must be silent, flexible, and creative in our thinking to seek God's will. Seniors have spent the first half of their lives working within a career setting. After retirement from the world of work, a calling is more likely because we are no longer following the will of our boss, family, negative thoughts, etc. We are free to open up our minds to the endless possibilities that await us and require only our time and imagination.

Child-like: To see the world through the eyes of a child is to embrace the sense of wonder in everything new. Our adult years are filled with "have tos" that chain us into lifestyles that stifle creativity and growth. Children (as Robert Kennedy once paraphrased) see the world as it is and ask why not? Joy and wonder are two sides of the same coin. We have a choice after drawing our last paycheck—we can rely on social security to take care of us and exist in a rut which is no more than an open grave, or we can thrive with the belief that anything is possible if we open ourselves to the why nots?

Sharing: Somewhere along the way we lost our capacity for sharing. As children we were taught to share our toys and time with playmates. Adulthood and competition pushed us into another paradigm of selfishness and loneliness. The myth of the "self-made man" is another stereotype pushed by Hollywood in the thirties (vintage Fonda and *The Grapes of Wrath*) that independence is the key to survival. To think otherwise would be antithetical to democracy and the American way of life. Isn't it interesting that after retirement we become playmates again through RV clubs, vacation clubs, church socials, volunteering, mentoring, and continued education? Support groups have become quite popular among seniors as evidenced by the prolific growth of communal senior housing alternatives, entertainment, and social events.

Demonstrative: Before the Boomers, seniors were portrayed by the media as wimps, fools, gullible, and easy targets for scams. Now most of the emails I receive about scams come from seniors policing their emails for the latest scam and alerting their adult children. I pity the poor phone marketer calling grandma and grandpa today. First they won't get anyone on a land line. Seniors are now wired to the Internet with laptops, cell phones, Bluetooth, and Blackberries. Seniors are savvy to scammers and spammers and are quick to report them to BBB or the Attorney General's office. No more Mr. and Mrs. Nice Guys for the Boomers. They know what they want and their precious time will not be usurped by some insipid telephone or Internet marketer. As Kathy Bates once said in a Hollywood movie, "I'm older and have more insurance."

Disciplined: The Boomers today are among the most formally educated generation. We began our educational careers in portable first grade classrooms because of the large post-World War II birthrates. We continued our education beyond college to achieve some of the most advanced education. Apart from the sheer volume of knowledge assimilated into our synapses we have disciplined ourselves to follow through on our commitments to ourselves and others. Generation X and XY are too self-indulgent to know the meaning of discipline, and we, their parents, or partially to blame for giving them the illusion that we are placed on this earth to be entertained rather than to assimilate and share knowledge with one another. It's no surprise that the drop-out rate in our military boot camps today is at an all time high and elite units are desperate for men and women who excel in discipline. It's this same discipline that will allow seniors to take charge of their future and not leave our decisions to phone marketers.

Resolute: A close cousin to discipline is an assuredness that we are the masters of our own fate. Without taking anything away from the spiritual calling discussed earlier, we have free will to embark on any endeavor we choose. As Boomers we grew up in families where discipline was strongly enforced. Our parents were resolute in their determination to send us to college and make us independent. Eighteen was the magic age for ejection and entry into the real world. Now kids watch "reality shows" on TV for a glimpse of what Hollywood believes is the real world. Resolute is all about being decisive, bold, persevering, and disciplined. No wonder that leadership flourishes in American companies today because of Boomers who have advanced to CEO positions and are determined to follow the course set by the Boards of Directors. But be aware of a potential talent drain once the Boomers begin to retire from corporate life. Our children have grown up in a world of make believe and we may be forced to look to other countries for CEOs to lead American companies.

Gifted: I'm using the word gifted to mean talented as contrasted with innovative which is more future-directed. In many ways gifted is the summation of the previous adjectives used to describe today's Boomer who is on the verge of retirement. SCORE (Service Corps of Retired Executives) is an organization that has consistently given of their talents and skills to younger executives through mentoring, coaching, consulting, or volunteering their time and energy to budding entrepreneurs or business executives. Many of our "retired" executives now sit on Boards of Directors, serve as adjunct faculty, and give to many philanthropic organizations that further opportunities for the next wave of retirees. We have open-sourced our lives in a world of proprietary patents, trademarks, and copyrights. We view the world as composed of finite resources that when depleted will begin to adulterate the talent drain to other countries that is already occurring.

The theme of this chapter began with "let me thrive," after using a movie vignette from *Failure to Launch*. The Boomers of today have both an obligation and duty to continue to offer their talent and vision in the same vein our ancestors have for generations. Part of that responsibility is making the tough choices that promote growth and learning instead of stagnation and resignation. Although *Failure to Launch* was a theatrical rendition of what is happening to our Generation XY, we Boomers can ill afford to fail to launch the next generation into a world that will become even more complex, ambiguous, and fearful. Drawing inside the lines, while popular in the sixties and seventies, will create even a larger intellectual deficit that will overcome the trade deficit that now exists. Our only recourse is to believe in ourselves and our ability to learn, teach, and grow in our pursuit of knowledge until we are set free at last.

19

I'm Not Old, I'm Bold

I've often wondered what it would be like to get another chance at what you do best. Many of us corporate types generally peak in our forties and hit the "glass ceiling" and then try to hold onto our jobs until either a layoff or severance package. While watching the Masters Golf tournament yesterday I was reminded that golfers peak in their thirties as attested by the leader board until 38-year old Phil Michelson won his second green jacket. It was refreshing but somewhat sad to see Ben Crenshaw at 54 years old finish up at plus 11 for the tournament. He was gracious and you could tell that he was not up to challenging the lengthening of the course at Augusta. I remember watching Ben and Tom (Kite) as seniors in high school in Austin, Texas, perfecting their game at the Austin Municipal Golf Course (MUNY) in the mid-sixties. There was no one who could out drive these two phenoms at 17 years and Ben still holds the course record at 59. They both went on to play for the University of Texas and did well on the PGA Tour. Tom would go on to prosper on the Senior's Tour (which begins at 50) while Ben placed his energies on course architecture and design.

Another memory was reliving the 1986 Masters when Jack Nicklaus won his sixth green jacket at age 46, the oldest person to accomplish this feat. Fred Couples had an opportunity yesterday, but his putting stroke was not there; he nevertheless tied for third and his swing is a beauty to behold—another Texas golfer who graduated from the University of Houston and was a roommate with Jim Nance, the CBS golf analyst for many years. Yes, the announcers can age gracefully without losing their touch with the mike, but aging athletes remind all of us that peak performances are contained in a decade for most of us.

What does golf have to do with corporate life, retirement, and aging? I think plenty. First, there is pure energy and resolve to win at any cost. Look at a young corporate lapper (laptop) at the airport the next time you're on your way to your timeshare. These guys and gals are "gung ho" idealistic road warriors who measure their lives in minutes, IM, e-mail, and cell phone calls. POD conferencing is now the rage and many are in class with no more than two earplugs and a laptop or IPOD. Youthful exuberance is a beauty to behold and the sports world provides a fitting metaphor for our work lives (after all sports is a job for pro athletes).

In the forties sitting in a college classroom or working an assembly line was proof that stamina and ambition were all that was needed to be successful in your job. We were supporting our troops abroad and the military-industrial complex was born. The fifties were a time of productivity with the auto industry and household items leading the way. Proctor and Gamble and General Electric helped bridge the gap from supporting the war to a peacetime economy. By the way, these behemoth corporations still are in the top 10 of the most successful companies in the U.S. today. The reason for their success is adaptability and leadership training. The sixties were a time of public service. Schools of Public Health, Think Tanks, Research Institutes, the Peace Corps, were part of Kennedy's youth and idealism and Johnson's Great Society, and young ideologues gladly disposed of their sheepskins to serve the greater good. In the seventies, cynicism and doubt pervaded our corporate culture, brought on by Watergate and the resignation of a president. The eighties were the "me" generation with MBA programs placing young executives in supportive positions to operations and the beginning of elitism and cronyism in American corporations. The nineties belong to the "Microsoft" era with the rapid proliferation of knowledge and proprietary software that changed the way business transferred information (notice I didn't say knowledge). After Y2K American companies began to lose their competitive edge to foreign competition in large part because aging executives did little to advance innovation and knowledge. They did not (as Peter Drucker said in an *HBR* article in 2004) practice effective management. In essence, they executives stopped listening to the American consumer (as evidenced by the demise of GM, Ford, and Chrysler); leaders did not take responsibility for their decisions (as evidenced the Enron debacle); they failed to do what's right for the enterprise (as evidenced by our unwillingness to explore alternative fuel resources); they failed to ask "what needs to be done?"

Back to our golf metaphor—very few executives get a second chance. You either produce or you're out. In golf, one can design courses, continue on the Senior PGA Championship tour, play in pro-am events, lend one's name to a myriad of corporate sponsors (as evidence by Tiger and Phil with Accenture, Nike, and Ford), or just retire at fifty. But what about the aging executive who knows he's (or she's) history and is holding on to a job defined by efficiency rather than effectiveness, by information exchange rather than innovation and knowledge transfer, and by managing rather than leading?

We've all heard the term "obsolescence" to define the failure of one' skills to keep up with the fast-pace changing technology and leadership tools necessary to manage and motivate people. But with the Boomers now approaching their mid-fifties a new term has emerged—middlescence—to define burn-out, bottlenecked, and bored "B" players who are below star "A" material but essential to the company. (see *HBR* March 2006 article by Robert Morison, Tamara Erickson, and Ken Dychtwald). With longer life spans and fewer severance packages available for "B" players they are faced with anxiety and fear of keeping a job that they no longer enjoy but are afraid to leave because they won't be hired in their fifties by another company. The sources of frustration are many but here are a few:

Career bottleneck: The Boomers are large and too many people are competing for too few leadership positions in companies. Next to job security this is the biggest concern of managers in their 40s and 50s.

Work/life tension: Medicare workers are caught between commitments to children and families at the same time their work responsibilities are increasing.

Lengthening horizon: The Boomers are not the savers their parents were and they face working longer to maintain health benefits and maintain their standard of living.

Skills obsolescence: We've talked about this before; at a time when mid-career employees need rejuvenation, companies typically cut back on leadership development programs.

Disillusionment with employer: This has to do with the wide disparity in compensation between the "A" players (VPs, executive staff) and the rest of the players. Also mergers, acquisitions, downsizing, and resizing have created distrust in the ranks.

Burnout: People who have been giving their lives to the company for 20 years are stressed and stretched, often finding their work repetitive and tiresome.

Career disappointment: Reality sets in after 20 years that our youthful vigor and ideals are not being realized or co-opted by our desire to just hold on.

The gist of the *HBR* article by Robert Morison, Tamara Erickson, and Ken Dychtwald is that companies are ill-prepared to manage middlescence because it is so pervasive, invisible, and culturally uncharted. The authors offer six strategies for revitalizing careers:

1. *Remove the barriers* to upward or lateral mobility by relaxing some of the company's policies and procedures.

2. *Find the keepers* just below your star "A" players and give them the special attention already provided to the star players. Send them to a management seminar for a week at a Business School that offers a more relaxed, campus environment.

3. *Offer fresh assignments* in a different geographical location or part of the organization. Bill Gates offered four top game designers an unlimited budget and their own off-campus location to develop the XBOX 360 over a four-year duration.

4. *Career changes* via global job postings that may be appealing to "empty nesters" who no longer have the family responsibilities they did in their 30s and 40s are being implemented by Dow Chemical and HP.

5. *Mentoring* colleagues by a two-way pairing of knowledge to gain with knowledge to share like the program at Intel where the partner may outrank the mentor. Mentoring is the best way to place the greatest number of mid-career employees in knowledge-sharing roles

6. *Sabbaticals*: Wells Fargo Volunteer Leave program offers employees with five or more years with the company and good performance reviews the opportunity to work for a charitable organization for four months with pay.

As Boomers approach retirement they have much to offer their present employers but it is the company's leadership staff who have the responsibility to identify and offer incentives to the "B" players who have a lot of energy remaining to give to the company. Don't leave this task to HR. Unless top management is behind the program and promotes it, the six strategies listed above will fail and the gap will widen further around issues of trust, motivation, and commitment.

So back to our aging PGA tour player. Remember David Duval? He came onto the scene in the nineties with rapid wins over a short-lived career before his game tanked and he left the tour. Bobby Jones was reported to have said that golf is played on a 5-inch square between your ears. It is true that golf is one of the most challenging mental games ever invented where shot accuracy and consistency is paramount to remaining competitive. These guys ARE good because they have successfully mastered the mental game of winning. Any one of the top players thinks he can win any tournament if he's on top of his game (I'm not overlooking the women's PGA tour, as evidenced by our newest golfing phenom, Michelle Lee, who at 16 years just turned professional).

So the next time you find yourself disappointed in your career or life's goals, remember that part of your discomfort is your failure to have lived up to your youthful ideals and ambitions. Also remember the havoc that "burnout" can play in your life. Take time off for vacations, personal growth, and mental rejuvenation. Any pro athlete does this. Most have a life coach to assist them in balancing their professional and personal priorities. Remember to keep up your skills during retirement: attend seminars, take up new hobbies, volunteer, mentor, and take a class.

The Boomers will leave our workforce in large numbers during the next two to five years and the "brain drain" will be felt for another twenty years unless corporations begin to retool, retrain, re-energize, and reverse the trend of managing people to empowering employees to innovate without fear of losing their jobs because they didn't follow P&P or complete a timecard.

I began this chapter describing professional golfers and their boldness to perfect their skills and adapt to changing technology, that apply to those of us entering retirement. Think of your retirement as a second chance in your pro career. Rekindle the desire and determination you had in your youth and change the way you *think* about retirement. Do you want to just grow older or do you want to play at the next level? Remember the playing field has remained the same as the Boomer cohort extends their skills into their retirement years. Be bold!

20

Endings Suck if You're Mired in Muck

How many people do you know who lay on their deathbed wishing they had spent more time at work? Not many, I bet. Why do we get caught up in the corporate rat race that life will be (as Forest Gump once said) a "bowl full of cherries?" Go to any book store self-help section and you'll find the familiar titles: "Seven … (fill in the blank) of highly successful people." We're inundated with Western culture's delineation of success as a "win-lose" game. I'm nauseous when I see the infamous bumper sticker "those who have the most toys win." It's typically emblazoned on back of a Lexus with only 72 more payments left before the car makes its way to the "pre-owned" market.

We've played the numbers game since Old Testament theology. Abraham, Isaac, and Jacob were blessed with many wives, children, animals, priests, advisors, and they still messed up. Let's face it—we're greedy and selfish. The Boomers have bought the myth of eternal youth with every advanced tooth whitener, cosmetic procedure, and (name the body part) enhancement. In the good ole days, people were content to deal with plagues, God's wrath, anyone east of the Jordan River, and nature's calamities. Now we whimper when our new Lexus gets a scratch in the Neiman and Marcus parking lot.

I find it oxymoronic that Africa, the poorest nation in the world has the highest percentage growth rate of Christians and the richest countries in the Middle East are of the Islamic faith. We believe in "prosper-ity Christianity" when things are going well for us, but we're quick to question God when prosperity is replaced by poverty. Have you seen the sign "poverty sucks," with the kitten hangin' on the bar for dear life? Now there's wisdom literature for the Boomers. The only person I know of who kept the faith when the going got tough was Noah, despite his three friend's admonitions to the contrary. I'm amazed that regardless of one's religious beliefs (including atheism and agnosticism), we still rely on our own devices to outwit our neighbor. Nations do this and we call it war; ethnic groups do this and we call it insurgency; neighbors do this and we call it self-reliance (might absorption work better here?)

Granted I'm jaded after sixty years of clawin' my way to the top with a plethora of degrees, certificates, and enough initials after my name to make an alphabet shutter. The same Boomers competing for classroom space in the early fifties are now competing for Medicare prescription drug benefits. Nursing home beds are in high demand and long-term care health insurance is now the Boomer's rite of passage. Forget every-one we screwed over on our way to retirement; we now find ourselves with the highest risk of bankruptcy in our retirement years because of our refusal to give up entitlements given to us since the end of War World II.

Despite the gloom and doom, there's hope for the Boomers if we give up the "success myth" and gravitate towards "value driven" objec-tives. Rick Warren in his highly successful book, *The Purpose Driven Life*, alludes to core values that energize and identify rather than deify oneself. I have a few thoughts from my "A" list that if incorporated in your daily life just might move you out of the muck.

Abide: Abide by a set of rules that level the playing field—call it reli-gion, ethical equality, moral law, whatever. Some follow rules inscribed on two tablets thousands of years ago; others follow a stewardship mentality; still others have a set of tenets instilled in them from an early age that promotes fairness, equality, and morality. The important tenet is to develop a "moral compass" and stick to it.

Ability: There's no substitute for ability. Any person who ever made a difference in this world from Edison to Gates had an ability that drove them to ask questions no one had yet thought of or cared to think about. Too many of us sit on our duffs awaiting government entitlements to level the playing field. We cry foul whenever someone else seems more successful, content, admired, or respected because some immutable calculus dictated their success. Perhaps we should look inward and see what we can do to help someone else without reciprocity or judgment.

Absolute: Successful and content people typically live by absolutes. These can be religious doctrines, human laws, personal values, or ethical constraints that guide our every decision and human interaction. Absolutes shorten the playing field with a beginning, middle, and end point—no circular alchemy here. No snake oil, no cute idioms, rules, habits, or artistry to turn black and white into grayish sophistry that dazzles, confuses, and obfuscates.

Absolve: Gerald Ford's one defining moment of his presidency was his pardon of Richard Nixon, regardless of his guilt, stupidity, or corrupt thinking. Forgiveness is a much talked about religious concept but seldom adhered to in societies that want "an eye for an eye and a tooth for a tooth." It's much harder to walk away from a wrong that to try and make it right. Our egos and national identities become entangled with this dualism of good and evil when in reality only good and evil comes from our turning away from God.

Accept: Acceptance of ourselves in spite of our imperfections and motivations would put many therapists out of business. We spend a lifetime rationalizing our gratuitous decisions (good and bad) which leads to anxiety and a sense of self-importance. We want to take credit for everything good in our lives and blame someone else when things go bad. Life would be easier if we accepted responsibility for our actions and faced consequences that naturally would follow.

Adoration: To believe in someone or something greater than oneself is to remove the stigma of finite ineptitude. By adoration I do not mean "idolatry." We have enough of this in our world today. I propose that we worship a cause, tenet, law, or morality that brings people of all faiths, creeds, color, and gender together. "We The People" and "For the Greater Good" are two tenets from our Declaration of Independence worth revisiting and protecting.

Adulation: When's the last time you paid a compliment to someone without kissing up to them? Parental discipline and neighborly disputes could be avoided if we just followed the Golden Rule. There's nothing wrong with praise when it's justified and due. Too often our egos supercede paying a brother, sister, parent, child, or colleague a compliment that genuinely captures the acknowledgment of their behavior and actions. An entire field of behavioral psychology is predicated on this one simple principle.

Affection: Filial love is the love for our neighbor. It's a tribute that we live in a world with finite resources and stewardship levels the playing field from a myopic zero-sums game to one of mutual ownership and respect for one another. Agape love is love for humankind. The affection we feel for our worldly travelers on this spaceship called earth builds a sense of community and collaboration, rather than isolation and competitiveness.

Agreeable: What's wrong with "getting along?" There's a myriad of self-help books on how to repair broken relationships; yet, we have few books that promote "getting along" just for the sake of a peaceful coexistence. We can agree to disagree, but we do not have the right to push an ideology or personal agenda down the throats of family, friends, neighbors, and nations outside our borders. There is a fine line between Nationalism and Fascism; just ask any Jew who suffered Hitler's atrocities or those in our own country who have subjected themselves to illegal searches because of racial or ethnic profiling.

Alike: This seems simple enough. We are more similar than dissimilar. The last time I noticed my neighbor he or she did not look like an alien from another planet. They walked and talked the same as I. They may be of different religious, political, or social persuasions, but the bottom line is that we are ALIKE.

Amazed: Every major ideological or technological advance in our world is based on the fact that we continue to be amazed at the uncertainties of life and the unmet opportunities to make our world a place of construction or destruction. That sense of awe is crucial to combat complacency and blind acceptance of the status quo. Just because we live in an imperfect world is no excuse to exempt ourselves from growing in our faith, technology, and ideology.

Ancestry: I believe we cannot build a better tomorrow unless we are attuned to the sacrifices of those made before us. Every legal, moral, and social injustice was fought by the brave few who dared to question a complacent majority. Our country is built on the premise of first amendment protection and our strength comes from our diversity, not our demagogy. I don't understand why people today refuse to study history as if it were boring and irrelevant. Its irrelevance is derived not from historical fact but from our ignorance and pomposity to believe that we were the only people on earth to face the tough issues of supply and demand, inequality, nationalism, dualism, and any other "ism" you care to mention. Read the Old Testament if you think we're on the only spaceship called earth.

Apology: A simple "I'm sorry," would go a long way at easing tension between husband and wife, neighbor and neighbor, parent and child, brother and sister, nation and nation. Confession is "good for the soul," and let's our adversary know that right and wrong is a matter of interpretation, miscommunication, and hurt feelings oftentimes. Again, prideful egos get in the way of the Golden Rule.

Appreciate: This is kin to the above tenet, but is different in that appreciating individual differences leads to a greater understanding of our mutuality and common ancestry. Divide and conquer is as old as Abraham and the United Nations today is symbolic of our mutuality of shared finite resources on this planet called Earth. The farce is that countries are ruled by people with voices loud enough to be heard over the cries of the masses. National agendas become adulterated by individual agendas under the guise of democracy or dictatorships. Agape love is to appreciate that we all breathe the same air and aspire to opportunities for growth and encouragement.

Audacious: If change is to occur then leadership comes from courage to ask difficult questions that sometimes threaten the status quo. We have brains for a reason and that gives us the responsibility to move forward in our quest for retirement. Instead of sitting in a rocking chair and telling war stories we owe the next generation a greater appreciation of our aptitude and fortitude to "keep on keeping on." The Greatest Generation as Brokaw suggests was the Boomer's parents who fought and survived World War II. What legacy to we Boomers wish to leave for our children? Will it be "if it feels good do it?" Or will we have the courage to say "we can still keep it together to advance knowledge, appreciate beauty, and accept our fellow human being."

I began this chapter with Endings, but if we subscribe to the "As" mentioned above, we can form new Beginnings. Years ago there was a management article written about "muddling through." It had to do

with maintaining the status quo and shying away from the tough decisions that beg for innovation, resilience, and authenticity. May I suggest that we Boomers are called to NOT retire, but to ADVANCE to
another chapter in our lives that is based on the above tenets. Legacies
are built on forward movement. Retirement has too long been associated with a RETREAT from the world of work; it's time to get out of
the muck.

Epilogue

So after all is said and done, what is it about this "retirement business" that bewilders and scares we mortals who want to live forever. Change is inevitable and philosophers have debated developmental stages since time began. Eric Erickson, a Freudian ego-psychologist posited his eight stages of human life with the last stage being integrity versus despair. There is in Celtic mythology the notion of "thin places" in the universe, where the visible and invisible world come into their closest proximity. To seek such places is the vocation for the wise and the good. Looking at retirement in this context places gives us pause for our disappointments and our blessings. Both are inevitable truths that affect all humans.

I've tried to use humor to take a look at ourselves and to embrace the blemishes and blessings that we all embrace. Parting from one stage and entering unchartered waters can be challenging but if we view these "passages" as "thin" places that intersect both suffering and blessings then we can appreciate this delicate balance. We began our discourse with retiring from work and finding something meaningful to fill the void—to help make sense of our identity, and give substance to this life of ours. The problem is that retirement should be viewed as a noun and not a verb. To retire is to withdraw, to secede, and to abdicate our responsibilities. And that is just not true.

Our Boomers today may be slowing down, but we're not giving up. We have much to offer our children and grandchildren like generations before us. As the dissemination of information accelerates and our minds begin to deteriorate, we are left with enough gray matter to decide what we wish to do with our time, talents, and resources. And many seniors are doing this already—by volunteering, mentoring, assisting, and helping others. I hope my thoughts about retirement have been uplifting and not despairing. My intent was to use our thirst for knowledge to learn new skills, meet different people, and venture outside our comfort zones to be of service to the wider community.

The post-World II children have indeed experienced many changes from Sputnik, the first lunar landing, the space shuttle, and space station. From polio vaccines to cloning, from airplanes to rockets, from slide rulers to IPODs, from outdoor drive-in movies to playing DVDs on your laptops, we have been a part of an "information age" that continues to explode and surround us with information at our fingertips.

Retirement belongs to those who make the decision to leave the bullet train of life and put down roots at the next station. For many, this is the right decision, and they should not be second-guessed, for they have earned their "place in the sun." But for others we will choose to stay on the train that is speeding through life until that last whistle blows. And only then can we say with finality, that this life is done. And for those who believe, we've just begun.

978-0-595-44557-8
0-595-44557-8